WITHDRAWN

A New Look
at Shakespeare's
Quartos

STANFORD STUDIES IN
LANGUAGE AND LITERATURE, XXII

A New Look at Shakespeare's Quartos

HARDIN CRAIG

STANFORD UNIVERSITY PRESS

STANFORD, CALIFORNIA

1961

Stanford University Press
Stanford, California

Library of Congress Catalog Card Number: 61-6529
Printed in the United States of America
Published with the assistance of the Ford Foundation

PREFACE

THIS study constitutes an attempt to make use of ordinary and customary processes in the classification of Shakespeare's early texts. I do not wish to suggest that special circumstances may not have caused modifications of procedure or that the actual evidences of normal routine are in all cases adequate for the establishment of fact; but my contention is that when no actual knowledge about such exceptions exists, the probability of customary action should not be put aside in favor of merely hypothetical solutions. The test is whether this basis of customary action does or does not solve all problems that arise in the determination of the origin and interrelations of the early texts under consideration. No Shakespeare scholar would deny the importance of correct textual criticism, but it is unfortunate that in pointing out error and confusion, it is necessary to describe the origin and nature of certain fallacies and oversights, since no offense or detraction is even remotely intended.

The errors are for the most part errors in method, in particular the current method of inventing special hypotheses to account for unsolved problems. This practice, however, need not be permanently damaging to Shakespeare's texts, since it still allows the student freedom of choice; so that when judgment and training point to proper choices, the harm is not great. Most of the trouble comes from the establishment of conclusions on the basis of immature research; whereas the proper course is to hold these, often fanciful, hypotheses in abeyance until they have been completely tested to make sure they rest on fact. The precedent set by the greater scientists of our time tells us that even well-established scientific principles should be regarded merely as working bases for use in the further search for truth. What we need is actual knowledge and careful thought rather than speculation leading to unproductive debate.

I wish to make grateful acknowledgment of my indebtedness to three of my former pupils for the use I have made of their investigations: Dr. William Bracy, Dr. Grace Seiler, and Professor L. A. Cummings.

H. C.

Columbia, Missouri
September 8, 1960

CONTENTS

PREFACE   v

CHAPTER 1.   CLASSIFICATION AND MISCLASSI-
             FICATION   1

             King Lear—Pericles—Troilus and Cressida—
             Other Instances of Possible Simple Misclassifi-
             cation

CHAPTER 2.   SOME EFFECTS OF ERRONEOUS
             OR IMPERFECT THEORIES   53

             Romeo and Juliet—The Merry Wives of Wind-
             *sor—Hamlet—*Other Quartos in Dispute

CHAPTER 3.   INADEQUATE METHODOLOGY IN
             TEXTUAL CRITICISM   90

             Typical Cases: *Romeo and Juliet—*
             Richard II—King Lear; Other Problems:
             Love's Labour's Lost—Much Ado About
             Nothing—The Merchant of Venice—A Mid-
             *summer-Night's Dream—Richard III—*The
             Henry IV Plays

NOTES   121

INDEX   131

*A New Look
at Shakespeare's
Quartos*

CHAPTER I

CLASSIFICATION AND
MISCLASSIFICATION

I WISH, to begin with, to ask assent to an obvious division in the field of learning itself. One part of it, that of natural science, is tangible or at least manipulatable and therefore lends itself to experiment. By means of experiment the phenomena under consideration may be made to repeat themselves. The other part, where we live and move and have our being, is not in its very nature capable of scientific demonstration except, to some degree, in factual and material areas. This can be said in another way. The whole field of learning is subject to an inductive approach, but in the field of experiment, deduction, operating by means of the hypothesis, tends to take the lead; whereas in the field of nonexperimental or discursive subjects—theology, philosophy, the social sciences, and the humanities—induction is the ultimate reliance, and however much the inductive process may be interrupted and perhaps assisted by incidental flashes of insight, the issue must be kept open and the generalization suspended until the fullest possible knowledge and comprehension have been arrived at. Otherwise the inductive process is thwarted. The generalization of false or only partly true hypotheses splits the subject into unwarranted fragments, narrows the field, and breeds error. It may also be said that the generalization from a false or immature hypothesis blocks the inductive process, and the operation is no longer the search for truth, but becomes a mere deductive effort to fit objects into pre-established classes.

It is thought that in these nonexperimental areas convincing degrees of probability are the closest approximation that we can make to truth. But even if we agree with Bishop Butler that "probability is the very guide of life," the fact remains that the matter is relative, and the latest opinion of leading philosophers of science is that even the best established scientific principles must be regarded as merely working bases in a further search for truth. This places a stern limitation on positivism in the whole field of human learning.[1]

We in the humanities are, however, by no means helpless, although we suffer from an unwise formalism deductively applied. Our subject is sliced into periods and particularized forms, specialization in the parts of parts is the common practice. These and similar habits of scholarship create barriers against the function of our subject and lead to our avoiding the central issues. Such habits are unnecessary as well as unwise. Indispensable work has been accomplished, mainly, of course, in the factual regions of our field, by the application of the orderly methods of science— we have learned the value of dictionaries, abstracts, biographies, the accumulation of documentary evidence, the publication of texts, and the perfection of historiographical techniques, which are our main reliance.[2] But these are the tools of scholarship and not an end in themselves; in using them we should not lose the natural appeal of our subject and its social and individual function. What we need are scholars and critics of sufficient breadth and intelligence to make use of the facilities provided.

Unsupported theories and the misuse of deduction may be said to be normal hazards in the field of criticism, but our interest on this occasion is in a different area, one in which there is also liability to error. For there is no certainty even in the factual regions of our field. For example, records are inadequate and sometimes in conflict; the language and the ideas it expresses have undergone changes; ideals and principles, manners and customs, labor and amusement, even virtues and vices are not exactly what they were, and the words expressing them have lost or changed their connotations. This means that a past such as that in which Shakespeare lived presents a vast complex, and for want of reliable testimony we have before us an area in which premature deduction may lead to error of grave consequence. Of course induction and deduction are concomitant and cooperative activities of the mind, but the complexity is such that the completest possible knowledge and comprehension are the only safe road to truth, which means that the inductive process should not be truncated and frustrated by premature hypotheses and invented causes. It is nevertheless true that the supply of plays to the theater, their experience in the hands of theatrical companies and of actors, together with the acquisition of these plays by publishers, were processes whose controls by necessity and convenience form a normal or customary pattern that itself constitutes an initial probability. In other words, the varied features of dramatic texts may be made to some degree to tell their own story.

There are thirty-seven plays in the usually accepted Shakespeare canon. Of these thirty-six appear in the First Folio of 1623. Eighteen appear in more than one early version and thus provide an opportunity and usually a necessity for comparison in order to determine what R. B. McKerrow called a substantive text;[3] that is, the text that reproduces or may be made to reproduce as nearly as possible what Shakespeare wrote. The act of comparison demands in turn a correct understanding or definition of each of the texts compared in the light of its origin and of the experiences through which it has passed.

Unless the scholar knows the nature of each of the texts under consideration, there can be no certainty in the determination of the true orginal text, and there will be confusion, guesswork, and error. My own experiences as an editor of Shakespeare have convinced me that in the criticism and establishment of the texts of the eighteen plays of which there are more than one early version and of the nineteenth play of *Pericles*, of which there is one disordered early version only, there exists at this time a region of error and uncertainty.[4] Primarily we have to do with classification, and this fact involves us at once with logic.

Normal practice in the supplying of plays to the theater brought into existence two texts: the author's original or so-called "foul papers" and a fair copy of the same. The original might be the foul papers of a revision, since with both an original manuscript and a heavily revised manuscript it would be necessary to prepare a clean copy for submission to the censor and for the use of the actors. We waste no time on the silly idea that any author could or would produce a perfect original of either kind. Mc-Kerrow makes it clear that both sorts of foul papers found their way into the hands of printers, indeed argues that such versions were a main source of the supply of dramatic texts for publication. He goes further and contends that printers' copy was not stolen or faked up for printing, but was procured in various ways, doubtless because such copies were no longer needed by the actors and were therefore available. There can be no doubt that revised manuscripts of plays served as printers' copy for almost all of the good quartos of Shakespeare. These two kinds of foul papers, although disordered (the first kind in the composition and the second in the revision), were correct and perhaps with some difficulty decipherable. These processes account for many irregularities in printed quartos. McKerrow's contention was that these texts came into print because, being no longer needed by the actors, they were available, the transactions being in a sense commercial and not piratical. There is evidence that the dramatic companies in certain instances made efforts to prevent the publication of their plays and that as time went on their efforts met with some success.[5] Ownership was primarily in the copy, and the subject is complicated, although in the individual case usually simple enough. Fair copies, usually made for practical purposes, seem sometimes to have been made for presentation to individuals, and there are clear examples among both manuscripts and printed plays of the production of such versions.

In current practice it is usual to find described and accepted a third class of dramatic texts; namely "bad" quartos. There is no objection to using this classification for the sake of convenience, if the matter is understood.[6] Not many Shakespeare scholars, however, seem to understand it. There are really only two classes of Shakespeare texts—those that have been on the stage and those that have not. Acted plays as preserved reveal an unbroken continuum of stage alteration, ranging from the slight and relatively unimportant changes in good plays that have been on the stage, such as the folio *Hamlet* and *King Lear*, through such texts as those of *Troilus and Cressida*, *Macbeth*, and *All's Well that Ends Well* to the worst cases in and out of Shakespeare. They are logically[7] only one class, and if these plays form a true continuum, as they do, it is a violation of the logic of abstraction to cut off the worst four and treat them as a separate class.

There are three aspects of Shakespearean texts as they have come into our hands that will be considered in this and the two succeeding chapters: (1) simple classification and misclassification, (2) erroneous or incomplete contexts of generalization, and (3) a variant of the second category that may be described as inadequate methodology. First, however, since there are many interrelations among the plays to be considered, it is necessary to go somewhat further in the explanation of matters pertaining to the plays of which there are two versions.

It is obvious that after centuries of research a great deal is known about Shakespeare, his environment and his poetry. It is also obvious that to scholars of diligence what Shakespeare actually wrote becomes a matter of importance. Various circumstances to be detailed later make it difficult, sometimes impossible, to restore his texts with certainty to their original form, but one can say at least that the criticism of Shakespeare's text has engaged the efforts of many eminent scholars. One general effort in our own time is of the greatest importance and demands immediate consideration.

Procedure from effect to cause is the typical argument of inductive reasoning and is the means by which historians and archaeologists have made such conspicuous advances particularly during the last half-century or more.[8] It used to be called the argument from sign and has its popular use in the fingerprint. One scholar in the first quarter of this century, A. W. Pollard, had the genius to see not only that Shakespeare's texts have signa in their printed forms but also that procedure from effect to cause is the only road to truth in textual criticism. The importance of this method is that it may reveal the origin and history of the text under examination; for, as we shall see, the determination of the original text rests on correct classification.

Pollard's discovery, because it was epistemologically correct, put new life into the study of Shakespeare, and the method continues to be practiced, and in certain cases with a high degree of accuracy and success. The bibliographical method in its inception was an example of logical procedure from effect to cause, which is merely and properly an inductive approach in the search for truth. On the other hand, the argument from effect to cause has great liability to error and has for that reason long been under attack by positivistic philosophers of science. It is noteworthy that symbolic logic has come strongly to the defense of induction, so that no humanistic scholar can afford at this time to neglect the principles of the new logic, which not only has strengthened the inductive approach to truth in factual areas, but has made important advances toward sound reasoning at high levels of abstraction. The point of first attack by symbolic logicians is that of abstraction or classification. Symbolic logic revamps or restates the rules determining the validity of abstractions. On the basis of Peano's discovery that the copula of the proposition does not always mean identity, but often means "belongs to the class of," the new logic has been able to render the criteria of generalization highly efficient in practice. The rules above referred to are these: (1) The context of an abstraction must be pure; that is, there must be no incompatibles, no goats among a class of sheep. (2) The context of generalization must be as complete as possible; or, in practice, as complete as necessary in order to satisfy the instinct for truth, every possible doubt having been considered and rejected. In this final matter, the satisfaction of the instinct for truth rests on the relativistic theory of cognition, which provides in the presence of complete knowledge and comprehension an automatic recognition of truth.[9]

There are thus two ways in which classification may go wrong: it may introduce heterogeneous elements into the context (what Bacon called contrary instances), or it may not go far enough in the extension of the context. Add to this that the factors in the abstraction must be given their proper degree of importance. The second rule is of fundamental significance, since it forbids the practice of deduction from an unproved hypothesis as well as the introduction of invented causes. In general, it follows that the bibliographical method as an inductive argument from effect to cause is from beginning to end under the control of logical principles. Logic is the science and art of reasoning in all departments of knowledge. As a specialty its operation is not confined within its own boundaries, and there is no separate and distinct logic for the study of Shakespeare or of the criticisms of his text. There is merely logic.

In their handling of texts many Shakespeare scholars have for nearly forty years been operating according to the principles of the bibliographical method, which has been widely accepted and taught as sound procedure. And so it is if correctly used. It was, as we have seen, correct and beneficial in its beginning, but possibly because it was not fully understood, it has produced error and, as a method, has itself undergone corruption. We perhaps need to be reminded that work in discursive fields—that is, in those areas of knowledge that do not yield completely to experimental verification—is dependent on induction, and this in turn demands thoroughness and completeness. The bibliographical method demanded a close and intelligent examination of the markings on the face of Elizabethan texts in order to determine the classes to which they belong; but there seems to have been little recognition of the fact that the method was merely a revival of the ancient argument from effect to cause that demands for its proper use compliance with the logical principles governing that form of reasoning. Among these the primary demand is that the argument must be carried through to the end before its conclusions are valid.[10]

When A. W. Pollard issued his methodological study, *Shakespeare's Fight with the Pirates* (Cambridge, 1920), he had already published *Shakespeare's Folios and Quartos* (London, 1909). The two works are closely related. His work was sound, but limited in scope, since he made a bibliographical study of only four quarto texts—*Romeo and Juliet* (1597), *Henry V* (1600), *The Merry Wives of Windsor* (1602), and *Hamlet* (1603), the so-called "bad" quartos. When in the later book he treated these plays as a separate class, he included *Pericles* (1609) with them, although, as he himself stated, he had made no special study of that quarto.[11] He thus made an error in the classification of the *Pericles* text, which has none of the signs that had been used as criteria to identify the other four copies. He also failed to see that these signs appear in greater or lesser degree in the texts of all plays that have been acted on the stage.

Pollard was a pioneer in the field and a conservative and perspicacious scholar. He had the ability to see the only road to truth in this highly complicated area; namely, the argument from effect to cause. But when he came to interpret his findings—that is, to account for the badness of the "bad" quartos—the context of his generalization was inadequate in that he failed to give proper weight to the vast deterioration that plays underwent when they were acted on the stage. He also stopped too soon and thus limited the extension of his context. On the basis of the four corrupt texts examined, Pollard in his later book put forward the hypothesis that dishonest actors had made copies of these plays and sold them to dishonest printers. This conjecture was well received, but its inadequacy was soon apparent. It lacked testimony or any actual evidence in its favor, did injustice to both players and printers, and besides these weaknesses overlooked a special feature of importance. The quartos of *Hamlet*, *The Merry Wives of Windsor*, and *Romeo and Juliet* were certainly printed from prompt-books, so that if they were dishonestly come by, it was with a view to unauthorized acting and not printing. The quarto of *Henry V* lacks these marks.[12]

Pollard's classification was premature, since it did not rest on the investigation of the whole field of stage alteration but only that of four texts. This was at that time too much to expect of Pollard, who proved his invaluable main contention that there are good Shakespeare quartos as well as bad. But since Pollard's classification was eagerly seized upon, the hypothetical establishment of too small a class did serve to stop the search for truth in favor of an *a priori* process of mere argument. The Pollard hypothesis, which was an honest one, was soon supplanted by a vague and even less well supported theory known as memorial reconstruction. The vaguer a false hypothesis is, the more extensive are its possibilities in the generation and perpetuation of error. This conjecture is variously stated according to the fancy of its users and the needs of the argument.[13] There is no recorded testimony in favor of the memorial hypothesis, and the criteria adduced to support it are all merely mnemonic, although it is obvious that bad memory affects revisers, printers, and copyists as well as actors and prompters. One may go even further and point out that no so-called reported version could be as irregular and nonsensically defective as are some of the texts concerned, since any text made by any reporter, however ignorant and unskillful, would be sure to have some sort of individual marking, some sort of style or lack of style throughout.

Sir Edmund Chambers saw the situation with reference to corrupt dramatic texts, and although he somewhat unexpectedly seizes on reporting as the agency of corruption, his statement will be useful in making the situation clear. He says with reference to the worst quartos:[14]

They differ in detail, and each presents features of special difficulty. But they have in common a measure of textual corruption, far beyond anything which a combination of bad transcription and bad printing could explain. Many passages are only intelligible in the light of the better texts which followed. There are constant omissions leaving *lacunae* in the sense, constant paraphrases, constant inversion of the order of sentences, and dislocations in the sequence of dialogues and episodes. The metre is bungled; verse lines are wrongly divided; prose is printed as verse and verse as prose. The diction betrays a substitution of synonyms or loose verbal equivalents or variant inflections, for the reading intended by the author. The total effect is one of perversion and vulgarization.

Chambers thus saw that the results are far beyond the sins of printers and copyists. Indeed, there remains only one agency so varied and so bound by necessity and situation that could and would have produced such results, and that is the actors themselves.

The situation demands consideration of a large number of plays, both printed and in manuscript, that have been acted on the stage—stage presentation being revealed by the familiar criteria of censorship, prompter's markings, stage directions in the curt style of the prompter, anticipatory entrances, shifting of roles, noting of music and of stage properties, simplified language, cuts for actor-economy or for the saving of time, names of actors or supernumeraries instead of names of characters, and some other features. In plays in manuscript these alterations are often made unmistakable by difference in handwriting.[15] These stage modifications appear in prompt-books, possibly because when a company was on tour and revivals frequent, the prompter had to know how lines could be and would be spoken. In any case the markings *are* in prompt-books. With these and the foregoing considerations in mind, we are prepared to consider the classification of Elizabethan dramatic texts.

There is, as we have seen, no evidence, even in the form of necessity or convenience, to justify the establishment of a class of reported plays. Therefore, until such evidence is forthcoming, there will be no recognition of such a class except as an invented cause and a breeder of error.

We are now in position to consider outstanding examples of the simplest group of misclassifications, those due to the impurity of the context of abstraction. We shall begin with the 1608 quarto of *King Lear*.

King Lear[16]

Nowhere is current Shakespeare scholarship in greater perplexity and over a simpler problem than in the textual history of *King Lear*. Adherence to a wrong theory is calamitous for the text of this great play; on the other hand, unsupported disagreement with mistaken theories is futile. It ought to be possible to proceed within the ordinary and familiar conditions of the authorship, playing, and printing of Elizabethan plays and, without excessive theorizing, arrive at a convincing degree of probability.

When Shakespeare began work on *King Lear*, the most obvious previous use of the Lear story was an anonymous play first mentioned in Henslowe's *Diary*, recorded there as *kinge leare*, and dated April 6 and 8, 1594.[17] It was played at the Rose while Sussex's and the Queen's companies were both acting there; but since the play does not appear in the repertory of the Sussex group, it was probably the property of Queen Elizabeth's men. This probability is rendered greater by the fact that in May of the same year the Queen's company "broke & went into the countrey to play."[18] As a probable consequence of this disaster, nine plays from the company's rich repertory fell into the hands of the printers.[19] Among them seems to have been the old *King Leir*, which was entered in the Stationers' Register on May 14, 1594, to Edward White. It is there entitled "The most famous Chronicle historye of Leire kinge of England and his Three Daughters." If the play was published near the time of its entry, no copy of it has been preserved. There is even a suggestion that it was not published then, for by 1605 it is probable that Shakespeare had entered the field with his *King Lear*, and we may believe that popular interest in the subject had been revived. At any rate, on May 8 the play was entered a second time in the S.R., this time as "A booke intituled the Tragecall historie of kinge Leir and his Three Daughters &c, As it was latelie Acted." Since the old play is not a tragedy and *King Lear* is, and since there is no likelihood of the old play's having been recently on the stage, the words "Tragecall historie" and "latelie Acted" have caused a suspicion to arise that the publisher wished to make people think they were offered Shakespeare's play; but the point need not be pressed, for the Elizabethans rarely, if ever, discriminated among versions of the same story. The heirs of Edward White may have remembered that they possessed the manuscript of a play on the subject of King Lear and thought it worth while to put it in print. Apparently they did not know that the play had already been entered in the S.R. When they had it printed by Simon Stafford in 1605, they gave it its correct title, but reasserted the claim that it had been lately acted: "The True Chronicle History of King Leir, and his three daughters, Gonorill,

Ragan, and Cordella, As it hath bene diuers and sundry times lately acted."

That Shakespeare knew this play is witnessed by a considerable number of passages that recall it in *King Lear* and by some parallels in scenes and characters. That he had a text of the old play at hand when he wrote *King Lear* is not probable, since the resemblances, although clearly recognizable, are not often very close, and since Shakespeare makes a number of casual and unnecessary changes in the plot of the old play such as might arise from a memory growing dim. Indeed, if *King Leir* had not been published and the manuscript was still in White's hands, one cannot see how Shakespeare could have had access to a text of the play. Moreover, such knowledge of the old play as he shows might have been derived (as has been frequently suggested) from Shakespeare's having been an actor in *King Leir*. And it may perhaps be plausibly conjectured that Shakespeare's interest in the subject came from the old play.

Presumably Shakespeare proceeded to compose a play on King Lear and wrote a considerable part of such a play in legible fashion and in correctly aligned verse. The old play ended happily, but there are some indications that Shakespeare saw the configuration of tragedy in the plot, especially since in it Cordelia, the good daughter, met her death. But that Shakespeare wrote a complete play based solely on the Lear theme cannot be said, since it seems probable from the state of his manuscript, which will be considered later, that a great insight or discovery came to him while he was still engaged in composition. The belated source was the episode of the "Paphlagonian unkinde king, and his kinde sonne" as narrated in Chapter 10, Book II, of Sidney's *Arcadia*. The story of the Paphlagonian king as told by Sidney is tragic in every line; that of *King Leir* is not, although it provides ingratitude, treachery, and suffering. The theme of Sidney's story is the evil consequences of filial ingratitude. This concept is taken over with its environment by Shakespeare and used to intensify the tragedy latent in the original Lear story. The obvious import of the tragedy of Shakespeare's *King Lear* is to be found in the story of the blind king of Paphlagonia; in other words, the tone, the setting, and the environment of a tragedy of filial ingratitude came from *Arcadia*, rather than from *King Leir* or from any other treatment of that plot alone. Sidney provided the stark cruelty, the filial ingratitude in dreadful form, the base deceit, and the dark intrigue. He furnished the theme of hunted fugitives, exposure to storm and tempest, a cave of refuge, inflicted blindness, danger, destitution, and, more than all, the deepest possible reflections on tragic folly and on suicide as an answer to the worthlessness of miserable life. These elements from Sidney's story not only furnish material for Shakespeare's main theme, but are, of course, repeated in the plot of Gloucester and his two sons.

It is obvious that in carrying out so cataclysmic and so exciting a revision of a work already well advanced, the manuscript would suffer in neatness, legibility, and form, and that these irregularities would appear mainly in the parts derived from *Arcadia* and in those parts that form a nexus between the Lear plot and the plot of the Paphlagonian king. If the supposition is correct that the manuscript used in printing the first quarto version of *King Lear* was Shakespeare's disorderly first draft, the text of this quarto ought to reflect the disorder and illegibility of Shakespeare's revision, and it does just that.[20] After allowance is made for the number of lines involved, we still find that misreadings, misalignments of verse, verse printed as prose, and prose printed as verse, and other typographical and formal irregularities are more than three times as frequent in the parts derived from Sidney as in the parts derived from the Lear tradition. This seems to render unnecessary, indeed impossible, the theory that the first quarto version was either taken down by shorthand from a performance of the folio version or put together by the process of memorial reconstruction, since neither a stenographer nor a "reporter" would thus discriminate against the minor plot, or could have done so had he so desired.

The conditions imposed by the situation required that a clean copy of Shakespeare's manuscript should be made in order that the play might be submitted to the censor and used by the King's company. In the places affected by the revision the handwriting must have been difficult to decipher, and since in extensive passages of revisional matter verse was certainly written as prose in the manuscript, one would think that nobody but the author would be able to set these disorderly parts to rights. The transcript, which became the Globe playbook, was extremely well made, so that it is no wild guess to conclude that Shakespeare made the transcript himself; it is hardly credible that the work should have been so well done without his supervision. Indeed, the folio text gives some evidence of Shakespeare's revising hand in the hundred or so lines that appear in the folio and not in the first quarto. Not all of these lines can be thought of as omissions by the printer of the quarto, or as actors' additions (such as Merlin's prophecy, III, ii, 79–95), or as adjustments for acting. Some of them, as Miss Doran shows,[21] are truly Shakespearean and are valuable additions to the play. There seems only one reasonable way to explain such revisions; namely, that a transcript of Shakespeare's original manuscript was made by Shakespeare himself, or under his eye. If we could be sure that Shakespeare revised the clean copy, there would be no doubt that the folio version has at least some original authority.

There is nothing overspeculative in the belief that when the transcript had been made and delivered to the King's company, it was marked by the prompter and used as a prompt-book, since that was a usual procedure. In the various stagings and revivals of *King Lear*, or of any other play, the play itself would undergo in the hands of the actors various alterations. Such alterations would, however, have a sort of justification in the fact that although they might supersede Shakespeare's text, they would often be more readily intelligible to an audience than the original. If, then, the first reproduction of Shakespeare's disorderly original manuscript was the transcript from which the folio was printed, it would follow that the folio was not printed from Shakespeare's manuscript but from a copy of it, that the transcriber may have made mistakes, and that the folio also in all probability underwent certain un-Shakespearean changes.

These conditions, however, do not invalidate the authority of the folio text, which was printed from a good transcript of a disordered manuscript and is, in some readings, a better text than that of the quarto. The quarto is not a "bad" quarto in the current technical sense of the expression; for when its errors and irregularities have been set to rights, it turns out to be our closest approximation to the play as Shakespeare wrote it.

There is, however, a simple and natural reason for this: in making a clean copy of the disordered first draft of the play, the transcriber (just possibly Shakespeare himself) had a great advantage over the compositor of the quarto, who worked at a later time on the same manuscript. Judging from the difficulty of the task and the excellence of the work, we may believe that this transcriber either had access to the author or was at least well skilled in the reading of manuscripts. We must not forget, however, that circumstances demanded that the clean copy should pass through a number of hands, and the region of its experiences is dark. In the period between 1605 and 1622, language and printing-house customs were undergoing constant change. There may also have been some authentic revision at the time the transcript was made. Such a thing would be natural. Although the revisions are none of them of overwhelming importance, they are numerous, and the possibility remains. The manuscript, having been submitted to the censor, was certainly prepared for stage presentation, and definite changes were made. About 300 lines were omitted, and there were other theatrical changes. We can also be sure that the text was altered by the actors in various small ways when it was played and revived. Finally, it was printed by Jaggard and Blount in their somewhat modernized printing style. Nevertheless the folio version retains much of its original merit, and there is no harm in thinking of it, in some of its readings, as a better text than that of the quarto.

To summarize, the folio has the following claims to consideration: it goes back to an excellent copy of Shakespeare's manuscript, is a much more orderly version than that of the quarto, and seems to have a number of revisions that could have come only from Shakespeare. On the whole, it may be said that beyond this point changes in the clean copy are due not to Shakespeare, but to others. Nevertheless, it is not warrantable to describe errors in the folio as inherited from the quarto, since it is not necessary to believe that the two texts have any relation to each other, except that they both originated from Shakespeare's manuscript, the one by copying, the other by printing. Common errors in the two fundamental texts, as well as bibliographical similarities (and there are many of them), are abundantly accounted for by a common origin in Shakespeare's original manuscript.

The only claim that need detain us here is that the quarto has within itself anticipations and recollections, and that therefore (since these features are used by scholars as indications of memorial reconstruction) it cannot have been printed from Shakespeare's foul papers. If there were any genuine cases of anticipation and recollection, they might have significance; but the cases cited are mainly localized and are of single words and short expressions. Nothing is commoner in hasty, or indeed any original, composition than this kind of repetition. As to the theory that some of the errors are due to mis-hearing, there are a few that look like aural mistakes, but could equally well be attributed in a work of this length to compositors and scribes. Some so cited are merely misreadings of handwriting, but one must remember that this error is one from which authors themselves are not free. Since these features have been selected somewhat arbitrarily as criteria of reproduction by memory, it has been argued that the manuscript from which the quarto was printed was a reported text. The possibility of producing from memory so long, so detailed, and, as a whole, so faithful a text as that of the quarto simply cannot in the light of the facts be granted.

The evidences of a revision in the text of the 1608 quarto of *King Lear*, a well motivated revision with all the disorder that such work produces, simply dispose of the theory that this quarto is a version reported by stenography or by any other imaginable method. Nothing but Shakespeare's foul papers used as copy by the printer could account for what we find. But this is not all. The original from which the quarto was printed was never on the stage, for it has none of the markings of the prompter. It is, moreover, the fullest version of the play, and when the blunders and misreadings of the printer have been corrected, it fulfills all the requirements of an original version. That the folio was copied from it is supported not only by custom and necessity but by the fact that the transcript underwent a certain amount of intimate revision in the process of copying. There is no reason to doubt that the transcript, after undergoing certain changes in the theater, served as copy for the folio versions. This is also in line with custom.

What more do we need? The 1608 quarto of *King Lear* reflects the characteristics of an original manuscript. It lacks all evidence of change that would have come from any kind of passage through any memory except that of the printer. The 1608 quarto of *King Lear* must have been set up from Shakespeare's original manuscript. It has been misclassified in the simplest order of logical misclassification. It is a sheep among the goats.

Pericles[22]

The play of *Pericles* has the following entry in the Stationers' Register for 1608:

20 Maij Edward Blount. Entred for his copie vnder thandes of Sir George Buck, knight and Master Warden Seton A booke called, the booke of Pericles prynce of Tyre.

The title page of the first quarto does not, however, agree with the entry as regards publication, and it may be that the copy entered and the one published were not the same:

The Late, And much admired Play, Called Pericles, Prince of Tyre. With the true Relation of the whole Historie, aduentures, and fortunes of the said Prince: As also, The no lesse strange, and worthy accidents, in the Birth and Life, of his Daughter Mariana. As it hath been diuers and sundry times acted by his Maiesties Seruants, at the Globe on the Banck-side. By William Shakespeare. Imprinted at London (by William White) for Henry Gosson, and are to be sold at the signe of the Sunne in Pater-noster row, &c. 1609.[23]

There were later editions in 1609, 1611, 1619, 1630, 1635, and in the second issue of the Third Folio in 1664.

There is also an interesting and important document, a prose version of a play of Pericles:

The Painfull Aduentures of Pericles Prince of Tyre. Being the true History of the play of Pericles, as it was lately presented by the worthy and ancient Poet Iohn Gower. At London Printed by T. P. for Nat: Butter, 1608.

Note that the title page of this book says that it is the "true History of the Play of Pericles." So far as I know, the making of a novel from a play is otherwise unknown in Elizabethan literature, but, as we shall see, there is no reason to doubt the truth of the statement on the title page. There are two copies of *The Painfull Adventures* known. One of them, that in the Stadtbibliothek at Zurich, has an epistle dedicatory signed by George Wilkins, a circumstance taken to mean that Wilkins was the author of the work. There is, however, one circumstance that shows that the statement on the title page is not the whole truth; for the author has borrowed considerable sections of his narrative from Laurence Twine's *The Pattern of painefull Adventures*:

Containing the most excellent, pleasant and variable Historie of the strange accidents that befell vnto Prince Apollonius, the Lady Lucina his wife and Tharsia his daughter, Wherein the vncertaintie of this world, and the fickle state of mans life are liuely described. Gathered into English by LAVRENCE TWINE Gentleman. Imprinted at London by Valentine Simmes for the Widow Newman.[24]

Twine rests mainly on the version of the Apollonius story in *Gesta Romanorum*; whereas the story that Twine's novel served to supplement, that of Pericles, goes back to Godfrey of Viterbo through Gower's tale in *Confessio Amantis*, Book VIII. This fact has some importance, although the difference in versions is not great except in proper names. In the play the hero's name has been strangely changed from Apollonius to Pericles, but in spite of this change and other differing names, there would have been no difficulty for Wilkins to perceive that the dramatic version dealt with the ancient story of Apollonius of Tyre. Indeed, Collier suggested that the popularity of the Pericles play caused the publication of the 1607 edition of Twine, and Wilkins's use in his title of the word "Painfull" suggests a known connection.

Wilkins borrows from Twine apparently both to improve his story and to supply information that he did not possess. In Wilkins's fourth chapter he inserts a description of the tempest that was apparently added by Twine himself, since it is not in *Gesta Romanorum*. The details of the wedding of Apollonius (Pericles) and Lucina (Thaisa) in the sixth chapter of Wilkins's novel come from Twine, who seems to have invented this scene also. The same applies to an elaboration of his source by Twine, the return of Apollonius to Tarsus, that was taken over by Wilkins at the beginning of his eighth chapter. The borrowing by Wilkins from Twine is often almost word for word, although there are usually minor changes introduced in order to suit Wilkins's purpose of retelling the story of the play. Wilkins must have known Twine's version all through, for these borrowings are scattered throughout *The Painfull Adventures*. But after the eighth chapter, according to Miss Seiler, borrowing becomes more frequent and of longer passages. This she connects quite properly with Wilkins's lack of information. It seems likely, as we shall see, that he did not work from a text of the play, but from the play as he had seen it on the stage.

If we subtract these borrowings from Twine from Wilkins's novel, we can form an idea of what Wilkins had got from the play. Of course the play embodied the Apollonius story, so that there is necessarily close agreement. The names are different in Twine and Wilkins. Most of those in *The Painfull Adventures*, not all, come through to *Pericles* as we have it. If this subtraction is made and Wilkins credited with making a fair report, we are able by comparing *Pericles* with *The Painfull Adventures* to note certain differences. We can also see how our Shakespearean play differs from the play of which Wilkins gives a report, and the motives that operated to bring the differences about. We can even get slight hints of errors that Wilkins made in reporting

the play, and I think we shall be forced to admit that the play
on which he worked was not, in spite of general and specific
agreement, *Pericles* as we have it.

Again, following Miss Seiler, we have no difficulty in seeing
that the Wilkins story differs from the story in *Pericles*. To start
with the differences are slight and mainly in the handling of
episodes; but when one passes a certain point in the action, and
when it is granted that Wilkins was (as he said he was) retelling
in narrative form the story of a play, the divergences between
the play Wilkins was following and *Pericles* become considerable.
The relation is one that can be reasonably explained only in terms
of revision, and it is *Pericles* that has been revised. There is nothing new or startling about this conclusion. It has been the opinion
of scholars and critics since Malone that *Pericles* is only in part
the work of Shakespeare, and they have known by the state of
the text itself and by the style of the writing where Shakespeare's
hand appears. If one admits the obvious and plausible conclusion
that Shakespeare revised an older play into the form of *Pericles*,
why not recognize the palpable signs of revision in the text of
the quarto of 1609? (Collaboration is the only alternative, and
the case for collaboration is inadequate.) The evidences supplied
by the text, in spite of the most ingenious speculations, can be
accounted for in no rational way except as commonplace and in-
evitable signs of revision. There are mislineations of verse, and
much verse printed as prose. There are substitutions or additions
of single lines, longer passages, and whole scenes; where whole
scenes are changed, we often have the testimony of Wilkins that
the play he saw acted was different. From the way the new parts
stand and are fitted into the discourse, it is clear that Shakespeare
had before him a text of the play he was revising. His revisions,
moreover, are more extensive than has generally been supposed,
and at least some of them may have been correctly printed and
thus escaped detection. If Shakespeare had taken fresh paper and
rewritten the whole play, the problem would be much more
baffling than it is. But we happen to possess, rather fortunately,
evidence of the play's origin; namely, a document that shows

writing in large patches.
e hypothesis that in the
was carried out on the
ditional paper to be at-

hical textual critics. A.
l" quartos and said the
e explained by the copy's
riters at the theater; but
special research on the
tolne and Surreptitious
ation, but seemed to in-
mund Chambers's brief
rehensive. He thought
regarded it as the work
quarto text, when set in
ters' errors, is a bad text
o fair comparisons with

irs is the more surprising
ument above referred to,
ince of Tyre. Being the
With considerable excep-
he Pericles story, really
the story of the famous Greek romance of Apollonius of Tyre
as we have it in *Pericles*. This fact is witnessed by general agreement and by verbal parallels between *Pericles* and *The Painfull
Adventures*. Many of these agreements were noted by Collier
in his Introduction to Laurence Twine's *The Pattern of painful
Adventures of Apollonius*. Wilkins amplifies his story of the play,
as we have noted, with extensive borrowings from Twine, indeed
with many direct quotations from him. He increases the substance
of the scanty Gower prologues as they appear in *Pericles* and adds
episodes not present in the plot of that play. When, however,
he does use the play, he does not follow it very closely, and
therefore it may perhaps be assumed that he had no manuscript

before him and was using notes based on theatrical performances. He repeats the riddle of Antiochus with a fair degree of accuracy, but most set pieces, such as the epitaph of Marina, do not agree with their counterparts in *Pericles*. He is perhaps closest to *Pericles* in the conversation with the fishermen and the tournament at the court of Simonides, but even in these episodes his version shows discrepancies. For example, Wilkins enumerates the six knights in the tourney, but mixes up their insignia and the places they came from. In telling his story Wilkins introduces gestures and actions that he may have seen on the stage.

There are many differences between the play and the novel, so many, indeed, that one is forced to conclude that the play Wilkins was summarizing was not *Pericles* as we have it. One clear and significant difference between the novel and the play is the management of the brothel scenes and the character and attitude of Lysimachus. Here we are able to see a motive for revision, and no revision can be understood without understanding why it was made. These differences and others to a lesser degree can be explained only in terms of a revision of the play of *Pericles* after and not before Wilkins wrote his novel.[25] The play whose story Wilkins repeats presents Lysimachus as a customer of the brothel, a circumstance that he acknowledges. The point of the novel and of the old story is that Marina converts him; indeed, the conversion of licentious men is her special aptitude. In the novel her eloquence saves her from Lysimachus, and likewise from various patrons of the house of ill fame and from a final dangerous assault by the Pandar, who in *Pericles* bears the name of Boult. She ruins the business of the brothel, and one may believe that this was a main interest, both comical and serious, of the old tale. This aspect of her behavior is not absent from *Pericles*, but it is there presented in a short scene, the fifth of the fourth act.

In Wilkins, Marina is offered for sale by the pirates along with other slaves in the market place of Mytilene and is much commended. The agent of a brothel buys her for 100 sesterces of gold and she is delivered to the house of ill fame by the pirates. Since she is still well dressed, she is sent out to be led about the marginal revision in many places and rewriting in large patches. These changes are explicable only on the hypothesis that in the making of *Pericles* an extensive revision was carried out on the face of an original manuscript or on additional paper to be attached to it.

Pericles was neglected by bibliographical textual critics. A. W. Pollard included it among his "bad" quartos and said the text was full of mistakes that could only be explained by the copy's having been taken down by shorthand writers at the theater; but he admitted later that he had made no special research on the text. Alfred Hart in his work on "Stolne and Surreptitious Copies" omitted *Pericles* from consideration, but seemed to include it among good quartos. Sir Edmund Chambers's brief treatment of *Pericles* is the most comprehensive. He thought the quarto text extremely corrupt and regarded it as the work of a reporter. We have denied that the quarto text, when set in order stylistically and corrected for printers' errors, is a bad text and are willing to submit the matter to fair comparisons with other Shakespearean texts.

This neglect by bibliographical scholars is the more surprising because of the existence of the unique document above referred to, *The Painfull Aduentures of Pericles, Prince of Tyre. Being the true History of the Play of Pericles.* With considerable exceptions, this novel is a fair retelling of the Pericles story, really the story of the famous Greek romance of Apollonius of Tyre as we have it in *Pericles.* This fact is witnessed by general agreement and by verbal parallels between *Pericles* and *The Painfull Adventures.* Many of these agreements were noted by Collier in his Introduction to Laurence Twine's *The Pattern of painful Adventures of Apollonius.* Wilkins amplifies his story of the play, as we have noted, with extensive borrowings from Twine, indeed with many direct quotations from him. He increases the substance of the scanty Gower prologues as they appear in *Pericles* and adds episodes not present in the plot of that play. When, however, he does use the play, he does not follow it very closely, and therefore it may perhaps be assumed that he had no manuscript before him and was using notes based on theatrical performances. He repeats the riddle of Antiochus with a fair degree of accuracy, but most set pieces, such as the epitaph of Marina, do not agree with their counterparts in *Pericles*. He is perhaps closest to *Pericles* in the conversation with the fishermen and the tournament at the court of Simonides, but even in these episodes his version shows discrepancies. For example, Wilkins enumerates the six knights in the tourney, but mixes up their insignia and the places they came from. In telling his story Wilkins introduces gestures and actions that he may have seen on the stage.

There are many differences between the play and the novel, so many, indeed, that one is forced to conclude that the play Wilkins was summarizing was not *Pericles* as we have it. One clear and significant difference between the novel and the play is the management of the brothel scenes and the character and attitude of Lysimachus. Here we are able to see a motive for revision, and no revision can be understood without understanding why it was made. These differences and others to a lesser degree can be explained only in terms of a revision of the play of *Pericles* after and not before Wilkins wrote his novel.[25] The play whose story Wilkins repeats presents Lysimachus as a customer of the brothel, a circumstance that he acknowledges. The point of the novel and of the old story is that Marina converts him; indeed, the conversion of licentious men is her special aptitude. In the novel her eloquence saves her from Lysimachus, and likewise from various patrons of the house of ill fame and from a final dangerous assault by the Pandar, who in *Pericles* bears the name of Boult. She ruins the business of the brothel, and one may believe that this was a main interest, both comical and serious, of the old tale. This aspect of her behavior is not absent from *Pericles*, but it is there presented in a short scene, the fifth of the fourth act.

In Wilkins, Marina is offered for sale by the pirates along with other slaves in the market place of Mytilene and is much commended. The agent of a brothel buys her for 100 sesterces of gold and she is delivered to the house of ill fame by the pirates. Since she is still well dressed, she is sent out to be led about the streets by the Pandar, who offers her for sale in realistic terms. This display of Marina in public is used rather skillfully to bring her to the notice of Lysimachus. He sees her from his window and feels sorry for her, really wishes to save her. It is admitted that he is "inflamed with a little sinful concupiscence," but he argues she will be better off as his mistress than if she remains in the brothel. His kindly motives are stressed. He uses his official position to secure special privileges, and there is a scene of preparation for his arrival in disguise at the brothel, a scene that, although not refined in any modern sense, must in the old play have been both ironical and amusing. Marina defends herself in much the same way as she does in *Pericles*, and although Lysimachus is at first sceptical about her sincerity, he is won over to a point from which he sees her as "virtue's image, or rather, virtue's self, sent down from Heaven, a while to reign on earth." The plot of the old play as reflected by Wilkins is neither stupid nor ill-intentioned, but it was hardly conformable to the ethics of Shakespeare. There are traces in *Pericles* of Lysimachus in the older role, but his conversation with Marina shows that his part may be interpreted, like that of the Duke in *Measure for Measure*, as an observer of his city's wickedness, but not a participant in it. He declares in *Pericles* that he did not bring "hither a corrupted mind" and that he came "with no ill intent." He curses Boult, condemns the place, and says other things that show that the reviser, unquestionably Shakespeare, meant to make of him an acceptable lover for the chaste Marina. The Lysimachus that Wilkins gives us is noble in his way and is repentant, but is defensible only by an older and a different code of morals.

This obvious difference in motivation and ethical standards between *The Painfull Adventures* and *Pericles*, as we have it, is a clear indication that the play of Pericles was revised after Wilkins rewrote it as a novel. These differing parts of *Pericles* have been generally recognized as Shakespearean and are marked in the text of the quarto by irregularities indicative of revision, irregularities that could hardly have reached us if the quarto had not been set up from the revised manuscript itself.

In Act I of *Pericles*, Wilkins's report of the plot is so faithful (exclusive of borrowings from Twine) that there is no ground for suspecting extensive revision, although in a few places disruption of the meter seems to indicate that the reviser has supplied occasional lines. Wilkins gives an extended account of the relief by Pericles of the starving city of Tarsus, which may indicate that the original play put stress on this event, and this in turn may add some weight to Graves's attempts to show that the play of Pericles (that is, the original play) was on the stage when Justinian, Venetian ambassador to England, was seeking the exportation of grain from England to relieve his city of Venice.

Act II of *Pericles* is also, in general, very carefully paralleled in Wilkins. There are a few borrowings from Twine, but exclusive of these, the resemblance in plot between the novel and the play is close, particularly in the conversation of the fishermen, the tourney, the banquet, and the wooing of Thaisa. This seems to indicate that the Pericles-Thaisa episode was presented in more detail in the original play than it is in *Pericles*. The superior style of Act III has caused many critics to regard it as the work of Shakespeare. This may be true, but a comparison with Wilkins reveals few differences in plot. There are again borrowings from Twine in order to supplement Gower and to emphasize the marvelous cure wrought by Cerimon on the apparently lifeless Thaisa.

In *The Painfull Adventures* the narrative corresponding to the Gower prologue at the beginning of Act IV of *Pericles* is greatly amplified from Twine with a long account of the death and burial of Lychorida, and some part of this seems also to have been in the original play. There are few indications of changes in prologues, but Shakespeare may possibly have revised them. In the rest of Act IV of *Pericles* there are clear evidences of extensive revision. The subornation of Leonine to murder Marina is different in Wilkins, as also the details of the attempted murder. Nothing is said in *The Painfull Adventures* about Marina and the flowers, a characteristically Shakespearean passage, and there are no details of her touching innocence. In other words, the important revision begins with IV, i. The contents of the brothel scenes are much the same in both novel and play, but the arrangement much more skillful in the latter.

Act V has been completely revised. For example, the contrivance in Wilkins by which Pericles comes to recognize Marina as his daughter is not ill-devised, but the reviser rejects it. In *The Painfull Adventures* Marina reproves Pericles for his obduracy in grief, so that he grows angry and strikes her. Her face bleeds, and she weeps and complains about her misfortune. This affords her a natural opportunity to recount her own pitiful sufferings and thus reveal her identity. The matter is handled more subtly in *Pericles*, but not with more interest or greater pathos.

Definite evidence of revision makes it possible to determine with some assurance the nature of the document from which the *Pericles* quarto of 1609 was printed. One sees that *Pericles* is not a "bad" quarto in the current sense, "stolne and surreptitious," but, from a point of view of text, adequacy, and literary excellence, appears to be a good quarto and the result of successful revision. In current jargon the manuscript behind the quarto would be called foul papers of a revision. The badness of the text has been greatly exaggerated; for most of its actual errors are due to the printer, and there are no major confusions and larger obscurities. The text seems worse than it is, because no quarto, except possibly the 1608 version of *King Lear*, has so much verse printed as prose. Some of it appears to be the result of marginal revision, but the quantity is so great that one is obliged to believe that the reviser wrote a great deal of his verse in the form of prose, a practice not without parallel in Shakespeare and other Elizabethan writers. There is, so far as one can see, nothing to indicate that the manuscript behind the printed quarto of *Pericles* had ever been used in the theater. The matter is difficult to determine, because the play undergoing revision had certainly been on the stage. A clean copy for playhouse use, and there would certainly have been one, would have adjusted many of the peculiarities of the text. It is natural to ask what became of the revised manuscript. McKerrow persuades us that many plays were printed because there happened to be manuscripts available, and I am convinced that there was a leakage of foul papers to the press; that is, of original manuscripts that had been transcribed for submission to the censor and the use of the company and were no longer of any immediate value or importance. However this may be, most of the verse printed as prose is in Acts IV and V of *Pericles*, where the changes in plot and character are most drastic. But many passages in the first three acts may also be revisionary.[26] It is precisely the parts of *Pericles* marked with signs of revision that have been universally regarded as by Shakespeare. There is thus in the *Pericles* quarto of 1609 an example of a play printed from the foul papers, not of an original composition, as in the case of the Pide Bull quarto of *King Lear*, but those of an extensive revision. What may have happened is this: As we saw above, *Pericles* was entered in the Stationers' Register to Edward Blount and was described as "A booke called the booke of Pericles prynce of Tyre." The second use of the word "booke" indicates that the copy entered was an authorized playbook. *Pericles* was, however, published by Henry Gosson and has none of the marks of an official copy. Gosson was in possession of Shakespeare's original manuscript, from which the fair copy had been made, and, by what arrangement we do not know, he published it. I would most tentatively put forward the suggestion that the official playbook was somehow misplaced and was not therefore sent to Jaggard and Blount for inclusion in the First Folio.

Troilus and Cressida[27]

In presenting a third case of misclassification, that of *Troilus and Cressida*, I shall refer the reader to Chambers, *William Shakespeare*[28] or the New Variorum edition for the facts of entry in the Stationers' Register and of publication, without, however, committing myself to these scholars' interpretations.

There are two early texts, one in quarto (1609) and one in the First Folio (1623). The texts of Q and F are very much alike, so much so that the likeness cannot be explained on any other hypothesis than that one was copied from the other. If they were copied from the same original, they would be more unlike than they are. At least this conjecture conforms with my experience. The texts run almost parallel for hundreds of lines with few differences except in spelling, use of capital letters, and punctuation, and these differences entered the texts during the process of printing, particularly, of course, the printing of the folio. (It is well known that Jaggard's printing house had its own style in these matters.) Which, then, was the original and which the copy? I think the folio was the original for three reasons: It is presumably derived from the authorized prompt-book of the company, the preparation of which from the foul papers would have been the primary task of the author and the company. It contains 46 lines not in Q, lines that seem to have been lost from the quarto either in transcription or in printing. And, finally, the folio shows degeneration of text due to acting on the stage, a fact that accounts for many differences. Nor is there any chance that either the quarto or the folio has been printed from the author's first draft. They are both much too orderly for that. All that can be said is that two clean copies of *Troilus and Cressida* were made, the folio first and the quarto from it. Why this was done is not known. A second copy may have been made for presentation to a patron or friend. This may be true, but so little is known about such documents that there is no way of following up the idea. One might, however, point out that the quarto as printed is without dedication or epistle. Two good manuscripts were made, one for the company and one that, if we may judge by the staying entry (the entry in the Stationers' Register designed to prevent publication), had fallen by 1603 into the hands of publishers.

The printing of the First Folio proceeded normally enough through the tragedies *Coriolanus, Titus Andronicus, Romeo and Juliet,* and three pages of *Troilus and Cressida,* which was properly classified as a tragedy (instead of a comedy as Bonian and Walley's absurd epistle had presented it). At this point the work on *Troilus and Cressida* was interrupted, presumably by Walley (the surviving member of the partnership), who apparently laid claim to the play as his property, a characteristically dishonest action, since Walley's firm had printed the play against the right assigned by the Stationers' Company in full court to James Roberts, and had handled the play in such a way as to defraud the players and deceive the Stationers' Company.

The interruption was a serious obstacle to the progress of the folio. Accident has preserved for us a leaf with the last page of *Romeo and Juliet* and the first page of *Troilus and Cressida* on the verso. The printers went on with the work of setting and printing *Julius Caesar*, but left a gap in the signatures and pagination sufficient, as they thought, to accommodate *Troilus and Cressida* when a settlement with Walley was reached. As it turned out, they left too large a gap. Apparently despairing of getting the matter settled, the printers procured another manuscript, that of *Timon of Athens*, to put in the place intended for *Troilus and Cressida*; but *Timon* is a short play and did not occupy all the room, so that the page numbering was thrown badly out, and other peculiarities resulted into which we need not enter here. Meantime, the printers set up the table of contents, in which they did not list *Troilus and Cressida*, presumably because they saw no hope of reaching a settlement and did not believe they would be able to include the play. But at this point, apparently, the way was suddenly cleared for the printing of *Troilus and Cressida* —whether owing to agreement between Jaggard and Blount on the one side, and Walley on the other, or to Jaggard's making good his claim to the book of the play by his having taken over Roberts's business, there is no way of telling. One hopes it was the latter. The folio printers proceeded to set up the play with independent signatures and no pagination, and when it was completed, placed it between the histories and the tragedies, or rather as the first of the tragedies. This matter will concern us shortly because of a peculiar circumstance.

As we have mentioned, the compositors' work on *Troilus and Cressida* was interrupted after three pages had been set up. The first page, of course, had to be scrapped, since it was the verso of the last page of *Romeo and Juliet*, and there is no record of it; but the second and third were, with the economy characteristic of the printing trade, carefully preserved. A time came when these two pages could be used, and they were. They now appear in the First Folio, bearing the numbers 79 and 80, the only pages in the play that are numbered. A significant question arises: which text were these pages set from, the quarto or the folio? Since they agree very closely with the quarto, it has been argued that the folio printers were setting from a copy of the printed quarto; but this does not follow, because, as we shall show later, there are several long passages in the play where the correspondences between the two texts are equally close.

Let us consider, first of all, the somewhat extensive omissions from the quarto text. Strangely enough, nearly all of them show some sign of being accidental omissions by the copyist or the printer of the quarto. The first of these (I, iii, 70–74) is a speech by Agamemnon in the midst of a longer one by Ulysses. The last word of l. 69 "speake" is repeated as the first word of l. 70 and may thus have caused the speech to be resumed at its next break at l. 75. The second is of three lines (I, iii, 356–58). The only suggestion of diversion is the repetition of "Limbes" within the passage. The omitted lines are, moreover, difficult of comprehension, a feature appearing elsewhere in connection with omissions. Q is also metrically disordered at this place.

At II, i, 67–83, there is a long omission, apparently accidental and due to taking up the dialogue with "nay good Aiax" (l. 84) instead of "Nay but regard him well" (l. 67). The next omission (II, iii, 39–43) is marked as accidental by the recurrence of "*Patroclus* is a foole" in l. 44. The last instance in this act (II, iii, 81–82) gives no clue to why it was omitted. Note, however, that it is a difficult passage to construe.

We next find three familiar lines omitted from Q (III, iii, 161–64). L. 161 is badly garbled in Q. It may be that the transcriber's or printer's eye mistook the first syllable of "Ore-run" (l. 164) for the "Or" in l. 161 and filled his line with the second half of it. Omissions are usually associated with confusions in the quarto text. For example, IV, iv, 79: "Their louing well compos'd with guift of nature" is omitted from Q, but when restored fits perfectly, although F has gone wrong in the following line. The next omission is, I think, easily accounted for. When Troilus, Cressida, and Diomedes go out near the end of the same scene (IV, iv, 141), "Exeunt" appears in both texts. Paris, Aeneas, and Deiphobus remain and speak five lines. There is another "Exeunt," and it seems probable the copyist or printer skipped the intervening lines between the exeunts. Another similar but less probable Q omission of some length (IV, v, 165–70) may perhaps be due to a casual mistaken resemblance between "enemie," the last word in l. 164, and "integritie" (possibly abbreviated), the last word in l. 170.

A one-line Q omission (V, ii, 68) probably arose from the copyist's starting the line correctly with "Troy." and finishing it with Cressida's speech. Two other Q omissions occur in this act. The explanation for the first (V, iii, 20–23) may be that the idea contained in "vows" and "sacrifice" carried over and caused the omission; the fact that "Cass." before l. 24 is omitted carries a hint of this. The second is a strange feature of F. It has been suggested that the folio text as a stage version had been provided with an alternative ending. The idea seems somewhat plausible, since, at a point before the murder of Hector (V, iii, 97), Troilus goes forth to fight with Diomedes, and Pandar enters bearing a letter from Cressida. Troilus tears the letter, and F alone has:

> *Pand.* Why, but heare you.
> *Troy.* Hence brother lackie; ignomie and shame
> Pursue thy life, and liue aye with thy name.

Before Pandar's epilogic soliloquy these lines appear in both texts. This of course indicates that the lines are original in their later occurrence; and therefore it may well be that F as a stage version had alternative endings.

There are only three omissions from F; they are relatively unimportant and may perhaps be regarded as losses in printing. They would hardly be excessive in such an enterprise:

> To others eyes, nor doth the eye it selfe
> That most pure spirit of sence, behold it selfe.
>
> (III, iii, 104–5)

Here the fact that three successive lines end in "selfe" gives abundant opportunity for accidental omission by the typesetter.

> And parted thus, you and your argument.
> (IV, v, 29)

There seems to be no suggestion of why this line was omitted.

> . . . rawe eies, durtrotten liuers, whiffing lungs, bladders full of impostume. Sciaticaes lime-kills ith'palme, incurable bone-ach, and the riueled fee simple of the tetter.
> (V, i, 23–28)

There is no ground for accusing either text of squeamishness, but these lines seem to draw near any possible limit, and that they were deliberately cut from F is assured by the fact that F replaces them with "and the like." The evidence therefore is reduced to a single line in Q that is not in F, and that (in any printed play) can hardly stand in the way of the opinion that the Q manuscript was copied from the F manuscript.

Let us now consider stage directions. It must be noted at the outset that neither text shows complete and careful annotation for staging, but that F is far fuller of the signs of the prompter's hand than is Q. The Q manuscript must have been transcribed from the clean copy before it was marked for acting, since the Q stage directions are prevailingly such as Shakespeare, who of course knew the stage, would write. F follows these in so far as they supply the prompter's needs, but often adds to them to supply the necessities of staging. For example, at I, i, "Enter Pandarus and Troylus" appears in both texts. The same is true of I, i, 91, "Sound Alarum," and "Alarum Enter Aeneas" (1. 108); and of I, ii, 1, "Enter Cressid and her man." At I, ii, 39, F provides "Enter Pandarus," but Q does not. This necessary attention paid by the prompter to the entrances of characters is usually observable in the folio; whereas the quarto frequently neglects them, especially when the approach of the entering character has been mentioned in the text. At I, i, 108, "Sound a retreate" appears in both texts, as do "Enter Aeneas" (I, ii, 199) and the other Trojan warriors successively returning from the battle in the same scene. At l. 261, F alone has the practical provision "Enter common Souldiers." At the beginning of I, iii, both texts have "Enter Agamemnon, Nestor, Vlysses, Diomedes, Menelaus, with others." Diomedes does not speak, and it is notable that F prefixes "Senet," since it was the business of the prompter to provide for music. In accordance with the same practice, F alone provides "Tucket" at l. 212, and has "Enter Aeneas" at l. 214. At l. 259, where Q has "Sound trumpet," F has "The trumpets sound," which may indicate that the trumpets were an organized feature of theatrical production.

The texts go on in very much this way. F attends to most needs of staging, giving fairly close attention to entrances and less to exits. After II, ii, 96, Q has "Enter Cassandra rauing," evidently the author's stage direction. F has "Enter Cassandra with her haire about her eares," quite certainly a conventional prompter's direction. To have the hair about the ears was apparently the regular way of indicating feminine distraction, and it was a special matter of costuming. (In *Richard III*, II, ii, 33, we have "Enter Queen Elizabeth, with her hair about her ears," her frantic grief being due to the death of her husband King Edward IV.) After III, ii, 220, we have in Q "Enter Vlisses, Diomed, Nestor, Agamem, Chalcas"; in F "Enter Vlysses, Diomedes, Nestor, Agamemnon, Menelaus and Cholcas. Florish." Here F adds stage music and also puts in the name of Menelaus, who, although he takes part in the dialogue, is omitted in Q. It was important to the prompter to see that he entered.

At III, iii, 37, Q has "Achilles and Patro stand in their tent," an author's stage direction taken from l. 38. F gives this conventional expression: "Enter Achilles and Patroclus in their Tent." At III, iii, 316, Q has "Enter at one doore Aeneas, at another Paris, Deiphobus, Antenor, Diomed the Grecian with torches." F prints this in practical fashion as follows: "Enter at one doore Aeneas with a Torch, at another Paris, Deiphobus, Anthenor, Diomed the Grecian, with Torches." This is originally the same stage direction, but the manager has chosen to have Aeneas carry a torch.

IV, v, 63 presents a typical case. Q has "Flowrish enter all of Troy." To this general author's direction the prompter has added in F "Hector, Paris, Aeneas, Helenus and Attendants. Florish." For his purposes the actors had to be listed individually to be ready to enter. To be sure, at IV, v, 158, F has "Enter Agamemnon and the rest," but in that case the Greek characters had been acting together in a preceding scene. At V, iv, 1 Q has "Enter Thersites: excursions." F has changed this to "Enter Thersites in excursions," apparently because "excursions" were exercises for which the company had been trained.

It is about as clear as it could possibly be that the prompter let the original stage directions stand if they would serve his purposes, but if they would not, he put in new stage directions or amended the old. It is also perfectly clear that Q was not printed from a prompt-book and that F was. F is full of indications that the manuscript has been changed by actors or managers to fit it for speaking on the stage. It uses synonyms freely; that is, words that would be more readily understood than those in the text of Q. The language is often made more colloquial, and obscure passages are more or less skillfully simplified. This is no small matter, for there are about a hundred such cases. One would think, therefore, that the folio text of *Troilus and Cressida* must have had a considerable amount of wear on the stage.

The great mass of textual differences between Q and F are single-word substitutions in F for original readings in Q; most of these substitutions are synonyms, to make for easier understanding, and some of them are mistakes: Q *broad*, F *lowd* (I, iii, 27); Q *influence*, F *ill aspects* (I, iii, 92); Q *sillie*, F *aukward* (I, iii, 149); Q *right*, F *iust* (I, iii, 164); Q *hoste*, F *mould* (I, iii, 293); Q *proue . . . troth*, F *pawne . . . truth* (I, iii, 359); Q *shall exceed*, F *yet to show* (I, iii, 361); Q *better*, F *worthier* (I, iii, 377); Q *attributiue*, F *inclineable* (II, ii, 58); Q *Prouer*, F *Creator* (II, iii, 72); Q *composure*, F *counsell* (II, iii, 109); Q *flexure*, F *flight* (II, iii, 114); Q *downe himselfe*, F *gainst it selfe* (II, iii, 186); Q *hulkes*, F *bulkes*, (II, iii, 277); Q *sooner*, F *begin to* (III, iii, 183); Q *once*, F *out* (III, iii, 184); Q *drosse*, F *cross* (IV, iv, 9); Q *my throate*, F *the root* (IV, iv, 56); Q *shrupd*,

F *hem'd* (IV, v, 193); Q *sleiue*, F *Sleyd* (V, i, 35); Q *sunne*, F *Fenne* (V, ii, 173); Q *strawy*, F *straying* (V, v, 24); Q *baite*, F *bed* (V, viii, 20); and others. It will be noted that some of the F substitutions are of superior elegance or force to the Q readings: Q *On which heauen rides*, F *In which the Heauens ride*; Q *vnslated*, F *whinidst* (II, i, 15); and Q *soyle*, F *soylure* (IV, i, 56).

One effect of examining these differences is to reveal, as might be expected, a number of errors in Q. In the following cases F seems to preserve the correct reading: Q *a*, F *another* (I, ii, 283); Q *feeds*, F *seekes* (I, iii, 267); Q *share*, F *weare* (I, iii, 368); Q *surely* (bis), F *surety* (bis) (II, ii, 14); Q *euery thing*, F *euery graine of Plutoes gold* (III, iii, 197); Q *to him*, F *to vs, and for him* (IV, ii, 64); Q *neighbor Pandar*, F *nature* (IV, ii, 74); Q *thy affect . . . earth*, F *that I affect . . . Oath* (IV, v, 178); Q *my Lord*, F *she low'd* (IV, v, 292); Q *finde*, F *fiue* (V, ii, 157); and Q *destruction*, F *distraction* (V, iii, 85). The preservation by F of the correct forms is easily explained if the Q manuscript was copied from that of F. In this connection will be noted such errors as the giving by Q of Aeneas's line to Troilus, "Neuer goe home, here starue we out the night." (V, x, 2.)

There is also a fair crop of cruxes. At I, iii, 357–62, there is mislineation in Q, which reads:

> *Vliss.* Giue pardon to my speech? therefore tis meete,
> *Achilles* meete not *Hector.* let vs like Marchants
> First shew foule wares, and thinke perchance theile sell;
> If not; the luster of the better shall exceed,
> By shewing the worse first: do not consent,

F:
> *Vlys.* Giue pardon to my speech:
> Therefore 'tis meet, *Achilles* meet not *Hector:*
> Let vs (like Merchants) shew our fowlest Wares,
> And thinke perchance they'l sell: If not,
> The luster of the better yet to shew,
> Shall shew the better. Do not consent,

This looks as if the passage in F has been set in order after Q was copied, but has lost something in the process.

At II, ii, 104, Q has "elders," F "old," and the original reading was certainly "eld." At III, ii, 98–99, Q has the unintelligible "our head shall goe bare till merit louer part no affection in reversion shall haue a praise in present." F reads: "our head shall goe bare till merit crowne it: no perfection in reversion shall haue a praise in present:" There is no literal connection between "louer part" and "crowne it," so that the F reading is possibly to be regarded as a correction. The passage can be construed if one reads "couer" for "louer" and understands "affection" to mean affectation or pretense. Q would seem to have the original reading in IV, iv, 123–24:

> To shame the seale of my petition to thee:
> In praising her.

F: To shame the seale of my petition towards,
         I praising her.

But this is by no means certain. At V, i, 58–62, Q reads:

> and the goodly transformation of *Iupiter* there, his be the Bull, the primitiue statue, and oblique memorial of cuck-olds, a thrifty shooing-horne in a chaine at his bare legge, etc.

F has:

> and the goodly transformation of Iupiter there his Brother, the Bull, the primitiue Statue, and oblique memoriall of Cuck-olds, a thrifty shooing-horne in a chaine, hanging at his Brothers legge, etc.

F makes good sense, and the trouble with Q is possibly the omission or misreading of "be" for "Brother." At V, ii, 11, there is evidence of the original in Q and a modification in F:

Q: And any man may sing her, if he can take her Cliff, she's noted.

F: And any man may finde her, if he can take her life: she's noted.

The quarto reading is original. "Cliff" is for "clef," and the reading is confirmed by a vulgar pun on "cleft." "Court" (V, ii, 118) for F "coact" is a fault in Q and the sort of mistake that occurs more usually in F.

Finally, let us consider the correspondences between the two texts. Disregarding punctuation, the use of capital letters, and, to some degree, spelling, we find that long passages are almost exactly alike. Note, for example, I, i and ii, at least as far as l. 261; also a long block of lines from about II, ii, 58, to II, iii, 21, and four or five other passages ranging from 25 to 100 lines long. If one overlooks a few casual variants, the parallels can be extended. It is therefore hardly justifiable to state that the first three pages of the First Folio were set from the quarto, since there are many passages of considerable length in which the two texts are alike. Moreover, these parallel passages at the beginning of the play, amounting to about 360 lines, are not by any means free from variants between Q and F. In the two pages of the First Folio bearing the numbers 79 and 80, 239 lines in the quarto, counting significant spellings, contain about 100 variants, which is not far from the general average.

A considerable number of these variants are certainly worth examining for their bearing on the relation between the two texts; for example, I, i, 104; Q *reides*, F *recides*; *ii*, 6: Q *Hee chid*, F *He chides*; l. 30: Q *purblinde*, F *purblinded* (e/d manuscript misreading in F and not Q); l. 35: Q *disdaine* and, F *disdaind* & (same as preceding); l. 60: Q *& ther's*, F *and there's*; l. 101: Q (*for so tis I must confesse*), F *for so 'tis I must confesse*; l. 161: Q *her her eyes*, F *her eyes*; ll. 152–77 (nine variants): Q *heare(s)* or *heire(s)*, F *haire(s)*; l. 181: Q *laugnt*, F *laught*; l. 194: Q *Ilion*, F *Ilium*; l. 194: Q *Cresseida*, F *Cressida*; l. 201: Q *lowde*, F *low'd* (possible mistaking of the word); l. 203: Q *I can tell you*, F *I can you*; l. 207: Q *hee's man*, F *hee's a man*; l 208: Q *iudgements*, F *iudgement*; l. 215: Q *that, that, looke you that, there's a fellow*, F *that that, looke you, that there's a fellow*; l. 220: Q *O a braue man*, F *O braue man*; l. 221: Q *man*, F *mans*; ll. 223–24: Q *thers laying on, takt off, who will as they say*, F *There's no jesting, laying on, tak't off, who ill as they say*; l. 237: Q *you shall see Troylus anon*, F *you shall Troylus anon*; l. 246: Q *Deiphobus*, F *Doephobus*; l. 251: Q *note*, F *not*.

I do not think I am misrepresenting the situation when I say that, apart from the actors' variants in F, the two texts are very much alike, not only in sense but in the details of printing. As already mentioned, it is a well known fact that Jaggard's printing house had emphatic rules governing spelling, punctuation, and the use of capitals; these stylistic matters unquestionably affected the physical features of the folio. It is nevertheless surprising how much of the style of the clean copy, best represented in Q, came through to F. But there is naturally a good deal of vagueness left in the subject of the spelling habits of Elizabethan printers.[29]

The problem here presented is less obvious in its solution than the problems of *King Lear* and *Pericles*, but has nevertheless at bottom a distinction between two kinds of dramatic manuscripts. A simple error in classification may thus cause error or uncertainty in the construction of a definitive text of *Troilus and Cressida*.

Other Instances of Possible Simple Misclassification

Othello.[30]—Both in the folio version and in that of the quarto of 1622, *Othello* sometimes presents an example of simple misclassification. The relation between these two texts is not, however, generally misunderstood, and the text of the play has not suffered greatly at the hands of editors. The most obvious fact that emerges from a comparative study of the texts of the 1622 quarto of *Othello* and that of the 1623 folio is that Q was printed from a prompt-book and F was not. Q has all the markings of a stage version—carefully provided entrances many of which are anticipatory, painstaking notes of properties needed in the performance, provision for off-stage noises and speeches, and adjustments to suit a particular company; there are also those modifications and degenerations of language in the direction of easy intelligibility that distinguish stage versions from authors' originals, and a businesslike syncopation or directness of expression appropriate to the stage. It should be noted, too, that Q has its quota of oaths and must therefore have been approved and performed before the enactment of the Statute of Abuses in 1606.

Stage properties and allusions to the physical features of the stage appear freely in Q and are rarely mentioned in F. At I, i,

82, Q has "Brabantio at a window," and in the same scene (l. 160)
Q has "Enter Brabantio in his night gowne, and seruants with
Torches"; at I, ii, 28, Q has "Enter Cassio with lights, Officers,
and torches." There is an elaborate arrangement at the beginning
of I, iii: "Enter Duke and Senators, set at a Table with lights and
Attendants." At II, i, 56, a Q stage direction provides for "A
shot," and in the same scene (l. 176) we have "Trumpets within."
At II, iii, 163, Q has "Enter Othello, and Gentlemen with weap-
ons" as against F "Enter Othello and Attendants," and so it is
throughout. At V, i, 47, Q has "Enter Iago with a light" and
F "Enter Iago," and at V, ii, 284, Q has "Enter Lodouico, Mon-
tano, Iago, and Officers Cassio in a Chaire," with no mention of
the chair in F. Off-stage noises and speeches seem in Q to be carefully noted, as in II, iii, 148, where we have "they fight. A bell
rung." There are a number of such cases. There are also in Q
evidences of adjustments to the needs of a particular company, as
at I, iii, 278 ff., where a speech of the First Senator is given to
the Duke, and in V, ii, 237 ff., where the willow song is cut as if
for lack of a singer. Also certain highly mannered passages do
not appear in Q, which suggests a desire to relieve actors of lines
difficult to speak. Thus Roderigo's sententious speech to Brabantio (I, i, 121–41) is heavily cut in Q (the speech may also have
seemed out of character for Roderigo). Seven of Othello's most
pompous lines (III, ii, 457–64) may have disappeared from Q
not because of the usual carelessness of the Q printer, but because
of an unpleasant weight they laid upon their speakers. To this
perhaps is also due the omission of Emilia's speech on the in-
fidelity of husbands, omitted in order to relieve the boy who
played Emilia of so long and so formal an utterance. It may
thus be fairly said that Q reflects conditions in the company that
played it.

Linguistically the relation between Q and F is both complicated and interesting. F is more formal and more carefully gram-
matical. For example, at I, ii, 17, Q has *chosen*, F *chose*, which is
slightly archaic and typical of F; at I, ii, 59, Q has *rust 'em*, F
rust them, one of many examples of Q colloquialism; at I, iii,

69, Q has *its*, a new form, F *your*; and at I, iii, 100, Q has *would erre*, F *could erre*. At II, i, 6, we find Q *ha*, F *hath*, such slightly archaic but still preferred forms being customary in F; at II, i, 28, Q *ashore*, F *on shore*; at II, i, 276, Q *which*, F *the which*; at III, iii, 306, and regularly, Q *handkercher*, F *handkerchief*; and at III, iii, 319, Q *known*, F *acknowne*. Neither text is without archaic forms, but those of Q are of a more vulgar or colloquial kind. For example, at I, ii, 4, we find Q *sometimes*, F *sometime*, and in l. 11, Q has *For be sure of*, F *Be assured of*, a simplification and directness probably due to actors. Q *where*, F *whether* (I, ii, 84) is typical, and Q *chiding*, F *chidden* (II, i, 6) seems to be an avoidance by Q of an archaic form .

The Q tendency to shorten, sometimes at the expense of meter, is easily illustrated. At I, ii, 37, we have Q "Not," F "And not"; at I, ii, 175, Q "I haue sir," F "Yes Sir: I haue indeed," which fills the line metrically. In I, iii, 189, Q "God bu'y, I ha done," F "God be with you: I haue done," and in II, i, 240 ff., one finds a complicated passage that shows a general tendency to shorten and simplify. Note also III, iii, 81, where Q has "It shall be full of poise and difficulty," and F, "poize, and difficult weight."

Let us now compare the omissions from Q and F. The omissions from Q are fairly numerous and amount in all to about 125 lines. The omissions from F are fewer and for the most part certainly traceable to error. The cause of the Q omissions is less clear, although error likewise explains a large number of them; in fact the Q printer was extremely careless in this matter. Taking examples from both texts, we find that the omission from F of "And in conclusion" (I, i, 15) is a careless blunder, and there are many such. The omission from Q of I, i, 121–38, seventeen lines, is revealed as a mistake in printing by "If't be" (l. 121) and If she be" (l. 139), the printer having returned to his copy far ahead of the place he was working.

The following are further Q omissions: "(If she in Chains of Magick were not bound)" (I, ii, 65) does not appear in Q, possibly because the printer mistook parentheses for marks of cancellation. The same thing may have caused the dropping out of "(Being not deficient, blind, or lame of sense)," (I, iii, 63). The loss of I, ii, 72–79, seven lines, is indicated as an omission by the occurrence of "such" (l. 72) and "Such" (l. 78). The loss of "I do confesse the vices of my blood" at I, ii, 123, is probably merely the careless omission of a parenthetical line. There are many such apparently careless slips by the Q printer. Now and then it goes the other way, and F suffers. Neither text can have been printed from the other. An omission of eight lines from Q (III, iii, 387–94), although there are no words or letters that may have caught the printers' eye, disrupts the meter, makes nonsense of Iago's reply, and would seem to be accidental. Eight lines (III, iii, 457–64) may have disappeared from the players' version because they were difficult to speak on the stage. IV, i, 37–43, made up of the broken utterances of Othello as he goes into a trance, may, as was suggested above, have been abridged from Q for the same reason. Two lines (IV, i, 171–73) omitted from Q cause two of Othello's speeches to fall together and must be an accidental loss. In IV, ii, 77–79, the losses in Q seem to be due to the printer's confusion over the word "committed." The thirteen lines cut from Desdemona's speech in Q (IV, ii, 152–65) may also have been dispensed with for acting reasons, since the passage makes sense without them, although they may also have been left out by the habitual carelessness of the Q printer. It is pretty clear that IV, iii, 30–51, and V, ii, 249–51, were dropped from Q because of the omission of the willow song from the stage version. Finally, there remains the cut in Emilia's remarks on the infidelities and inconsistencies of husbands, seventeen lines (IV, iii, 84–101), which, it has been suggested, were left out for the adjustment of a player's part.

The history of the quarto of *Othello* would seem to be quite simple. It was set up, carelessly, from a normal prompt-book, and since there was apparently no shortage of actors and supernumeraries and little evidence of abridgment as such, one would think that it had served as a prompt-book for a city company, probably for the King's men at the Globe. So different are Q and F in their provision for staging that one may conclude with great certainty that F was not set up from a prompt-book, but from a transcript that had not been used for staging the play. The stage directions in F are inadequate for staging. As noted above, many entrances of actors remain unmarked, and there is little or no attention to stage properties and off-stage speeches and noises. The stage directions of F are much fewer than those of Q, much less complete, and seem such as the dramatist supplied for his play. The language of F, as shown above, is much more literary and grammatically more correct and formal than that of Q. It makes few, if any, concessions to popular taste or to a low level of intelligence in an audience.

Q is, also as shown above, very different from F. It is not, strictly speaking, an abridged version like the manuscripts behind the quartos of *The Merry Wives of Windsor* and *Romeo and Juliet,* but is the text, slightly abridged, of the play as originally written. Most of its cuts can be plausibly explained as accidental omissions by the printer.

Variants between the two texts are numerous, F preserving, usually but not always, the original reading in significant passages. But there is no evidence that one of the texts is immediately derived from the other. In fact, in the light of omissions, this cannot be so. It is usually said that the two texts go back to a common original, and this is possibly a safe assumption. There is, however, a good deal to be explained. Profanity is removed with exceptional care from F—the offending passages of Q have not been merely canceled and patched; indeed the operation is so skillfully handled that one would think that the manuscript behind F must have been written after the enactment of the Act to Restrain the Abuses of Players (May 27, 1606). On the other hand, profanity has not been removed from Q, and a natural inference from this is that Q must have been used as a prompt-book before the Act of Abuses was passed, and also that Q could hardly have been used after the Act was passed. It might have served as prompt-book for the performance of 1604 and it could hardly have been used for the performances of 1610 and 1612–13. For these and we do not know how many other performances Q could hardly have served, F was certainly never used, and it would follow that the King's men must have had a prompt-book now lost. Perhaps the manuscript behind Q was lost or stolen after its first uses, and lay untouched for many years, only to be found or put forward by Walkley in 1622 in order to secure a share in the publication of the First Folio, or to derive some profit from the play before the collected edition was published.

One other observation needs to be recorded. Q has a good deal of mislined verse that has usually been correctly printed in F. Mislining is often an indication of revision, frequently of course during the process of composition; such irregularities in the handling of verse in Q may reflect a connection with Shakespeare's original manuscript, although in the case about to be cited (V, ii, 85–125), it is more probable that the irregularity is due to a change by the actors when the quarto was on the stage, the purpose being to dispense with one actor. There is an area of such disturbance in I, i, from about l. 50 to l. 66 in Iago's long speech. At II, iii, 54–57, a bit of prose is set as verse in Q, and at III, iii, 420 ff., Q shows a disordered text; also prose set as verse at IV, i, 127–29. None of these is of great extent or seems to be significant, but one mislined passage (V, ii, 85–125) may have greater importance. In the source of *Othello* Cassio has a wife, and Shakespeare seems prepared to accept her in Iago's otherwise inexplicable line (I, i, 21) "A fellow almost damn'd in a fair wife." In the source Cassio's wife is represented as skilled in needlework, and it is she who is urged by Cassio to copy the pattern of Desdemona's handkerchief. The Moor sees it in her hands. In the play the task is given to Bianca. In the disruption of the lines cited above there may be a trace of the story in Shakespeare's mind. It is possible that there has been a transfer of roles from Cassio's wife to his mistress. This is further suggested by Bianca's odd defense of herself when accused by Emilia (V, i, 122–23), where Bianca says, "I am no strumpet, but of life as honest/As you, that thus abuse me," words that would be more appropriate to Cassio's wife than to his mistress.

In general, one would conclude that Q was printed from a prompt-book based on Shakespeare's fair copy and later very considerably changed, if not degenerated, by its use on the stage; and that F was printed from a good, though not perfect, transcript of the clean copy of the play, or, indeed, from the original manuscript. This transcript was probably made after 1606. Both texts have authority, and they often supplement or correct each other. From these and other probably revisional features of Q comes the rather hazardous suggestion that the manuscript behind Q may, in a fuller and more correct state, have been the one delivered by Shakespeare to the players. In this case the manuscript behind F may have been recopied from foul papers or may be a transcript of Q before it underwent degeneration on the stage.

The Henry IV Plays.[31]—There is a manuscript version of *Henry IV*,[32] which is confidently dated as not earlier than 1613, the date of publication of the fifth quarto of *1 Henry IV* (Q5), and revised about 1623 by Sir Edward Dering (1598–1644) of Surrenden in Kent for private performance at his house. The manuscript was discovered in 1844 in the library of Sir Edward's descendants and was edited by J. O. Halliwell and published by the Shakespeare Society in 1845. It is now in the Folger Shakespeare Library in Washington, D.C. It has been regarded as a condensation into a single play by selection from Q5 of *1 Henry IV* and Qb of *2 Henry IV* of the two-part play as we have it.[33]

The manuscript bears no date, and the watermark on the paper (a pitcher with the initials P.O. and a crescent at the top) tells us nothing more than that the work seems to belong to the end of the sixteenth or the beginning of the seventeenth century. The manuscript presents a version of a single play about the wild life of Prince Hal, his relations with Falstaff and the Boar's Head Tavern group, the King's successful effort to reform his son, the Percy rebellion, and the rejection of Falstaff. The original hand is a fairly good, rather cursive Elizabethan secretary, and the manuscript has been corrected, edited, and prepared for playing in a hand that has been confidently identified as Sir Edward Dering's. Dering is thought to have prepared the play for amateur acting in about 1622. This date is to some extent assured by an accidental feature of the manuscript itself. Sir Edward in several places not only corrects the text according to some quarto of the play in his possession, but makes a number of additions to the text in verse. One of these consists of nine lines of new composition intended to replace and amplify I, i, 25–27. These new lines in Dering's hand are written on a slip of paper attached to the first page of the manuscript. It happens that on the added leaf there appears a partial cast of characters for Beaumont and Fletcher's *The Spanish Curate*, a play licensed on October 24, 1622. There are only two complete scenes of *1 Henry IV* not appearing in the Dering play, but there are somewhat extensive parts of scenes not in Dering, as also various shorter passages that are wanting. All these passages, in so far as they have significance, will be mentioned later. There can be no doubt that the Dering manuscript presents a play by Shakespeare, since its text is a word-for-word parallel of the greater part of *1 Henry IV* and of some parts of *2 Henry IV*.

It occurred to me many years ago that when Meres in *Palladis Tamia* (1598) refers to "Henry the 4," he may have had in mind only one play. It also seemed unlikely that in beginning his work on this first episode in the life of Henry V, Shakespeare should have planned two plays instead of one; for, seen from the point of view of the old Henry V play and other single plays treating of the reign of one king, Henry IV would appear to present only one dramatic subject. This idea was further reinforced by A. E. Morgan's suggestive and important study, *Some Problems of Shakespeare's "Henry the Fourth"* (1924); for it is obvious that if the parts he believes with good reason to be revisional were subtracted from the plays as we have them, there would be left just about material enough for one older original play on the reign of Henry IV. It is also clear that such an older play would cover the essential facts and be well unified and perfectly consistent; that is, it would tell the story of Prince Hal's unprincely conduct, his relations with his father, his bravery in the Percy rebellion, and his rejection of Falstaff at the end. The interesting thing is that the version of the Henry IV play as it appears in the Dering manuscript embodies just these features. We have a right at least to inquire how it has come to have them.

It has been taken for granted that the Dering version is an intelligent piece of cutting, which reselected the basic elements of the old story and organized them into a drama made up of these basic elements only. This idea seems an odd and unusual reversal of normal procedure. Such cutting might have been done from a recollected and reconstructed pattern, but one does not understand how and why such a pattern would have come into existence. For an abridger to cut out, so carefully and meticulously, all revisionary material is hardly likely. It is difficult to imagine what motive he could have had, or what prejudice against the excellent episodes in which the Chief Justice appears, or against Justice Shallow, a very popular character, or against Doll, or Pistol, or the amusing Boy. Lack of space might have caused a reviser to shorten these parts or to omit some of them altogether; but it would not explain complete exclusion, or the careful sort of cutting required to dispose of single sentences in the midst of comic scenes, dispose of them on the ground that they referred to one of the great comic characters introduced by Shakespeare in his revision of the play. No such modern Shakespeare scholarship existed at that time.

In conducting an inquiry into whether or not the Dering version presents the play of Henry IV at some point in its history after the name Oldcastle had been changed to Falstaff and before the drama had been expanded into a two-part play, one encounters serious perplexities; I therefore suggest that the first thing to be done is to discriminate between the parts of the Dering play that run parallel with *1 Henry IV* and those that run parallel with parts of *2 Henry IV*. To begin with, this process confines the difficulties to the former part. The latter offers no difficulty, since the argument of texts is of no value as applied to the scenes that carry on the story after the Battle of Shrewsbury, a matter we shall take up in Chapter 3.

The Dering version tells the complete story of *1 Henry IV*

as far as the Battle of Shrewsbury. At least two scenes and considerable parts of two others, besides a number of scattered passages, are not present in the Dering version and have been regarded as omissions, but there is, beyond this, no abridgment as such of the plot. The part of the Dering play, on the other hand, that is parallel to *2 Henry IV* differs in contents very greatly from the standard version. Of the parts common to the two plays the textual relations are of the same kind as those arising in connection with *1 Henry IV*, but, as it happens, are much easier to account for.

There are only two original printed texts of *2 Henry IV*, the quarto of 1600 and the folio of 1623. It is easy to see that the Dering manuscript presents, somewhat imperfectly to be sure, an earlier textual form of certain parts of *2 Henry IV* than do either the quarto of that play or the folio. This is obvious in those comic parts in which the standard version and the Dering version are parallel. An illustration of this will be given below. This relation holds true of the part that finishes the story of the complete reformation and the coronation of Prince Hal, but in a different way, and it is hard to see how the earlier portion of the Dering play could have a different relation to the two-part play as we have it from the later portion; for the Dering version is of one piece and devotes itself closely to the story of the wild youth of Prince Hal, of his reformation, and of the Percy rebellion. The surprising feature of this later part of the Dering play, as before stated, is that it contains no reference to the characters special to *2 Henry IV*—the Chief Justice (in his relation to Falstaff and to the new king), Justice Shallow and his household (with his magisterial importance and his contacts with Sir John Falstaff), the Ancient Pistol, Doll Tearsheet, Mistress Quickly in relation to these characters, and finally the Boy.

For example, and there are a number of such cases, consider the quarto version of *2 Henry IV*, II, i, 25–67, and the corresponding passage in the Dering manuscript. It will be noted that in D there is a mere quarrel between Falstaff and Dame Quickly, appropriate enough as a first version, whereas in Q the speeches seem to have been expanded. Fang and Snare are present, and Mrs. Quickly complains to them of her ill-usage by Falstaff. This scene is the only bit of Falstaffian material in the later section of the D text, where it is shorter but perfectly consistent. One can understand how such a scene could have been expanded into what we find in Q and F of *2 Henry IV*, but to believe that it is a matter of selection and condensation is difficult, indeed impossible. In practice the process of redaction does not work that way. This scene in D has every aspect of primitivity, and the process of expansion is the natural one, and the one in common use in all literature.

> *Fals.* But thinge; thow willt not lay a pewter pestle on my shoulders; saie:
>
> *Host.* I am vndone by thie goeing: thow art an infinitiue thinge vpon my score: thow owest me a hundreth markes almost: & I haue borne, and I haue borne and I haue borne; fub'd off & fub'd off, from this daie; to that daie; that it is a shame to be thought on: vnlesse a woman should be made an asse and a beast to beare euery knaues wrong.
>
> *Fals.* Peace kitten; or yow shall now in the channell.
>
> *Host.* Throwe me into the Channell: Ile throw thee into the chanell: Wilt thow: willt thow: the offecers ar at the dore to arast thee; thow bastardly rogue: murder: murder: ah thow hony-sucker villaine A thow hony-seed rogue: a man queller & a woman queller.
>
> *Bard.* Fie Sir John: doe not draw vpon a woman:
>
> *Fals.* Peace Lucifer:
>
> *Host.* Stab me in my owne howse: Most beastly in good faith: he cares not what mischiefe he doth; if his weapon be out: he will foyne like any diuell he will spare neither man: woman: nor child: helpe master Synok.

So far the D version; now compare the same passage as it appears in *2 Henry IV* (Q):

> *Host.* I am vndone by his going, I warrant you, hees an infinitiue thing vppon my score, good maister Phang holde him sure, good master Snare let him not scape, a comes continually to Pie corner (sauing your manhoods) to buy a saddle, and he is indited to dinner to the Lubbers head in Lumbert streete to

master Smooths the silk man, I pray you since my exion is entred, and my case so openly knowne to the worlde, let him be brought in to his answer, a hundred marke is a long one, for a poore lone woman to beare, and I haue borne, and borne, and borne, and haue bin fubd off, and fubd off, and fubd off, from this day to that day, that it is a shame to be thought on, there is no honesty in such dealing, vnlesse a woman should be made an asse, and a beast, to beare euery knaues wrong: yonder he comes, and that arrant malmsie-nose knaue Bardolfe with him, do your offices, do your offices master Phang, & master Snare, do me, do me, do me your offices.

Enter sir Iohn, and Bardolfe, and the boy.

Falst. How now, whose mare's dead? whats the matter?

Phang. I arrest you at the sute of mistris, quickly.

Falst. Away varlets, draw Bardolfe, cut me off the villaines head, throw the queane in the channell.

Host. Throw me in the channell? Ile throw thee in the channel, wilt thou, wilt thou, thou bastardly rogue, murder murder, a thou honisuckle villaine, wilt thou kill Gods officers and the Kings? a thou honiseed rogue, thou art a honiseed, a man queller, and a woman queller.

Falst. Keepe them off Bardolfe.

Offic. A reskew, a reskew.

Host. Good people bring a reskew or two, thou wot, wot thou, thou wot, wot ta, do do thou rogue, do thou hempseed.

Boy. Away you scullian, you rampallian, you fustilarian, ile tickle your catastrophe.

Enter Lord chiefe iustice and his men.

Lord. What is the matter? keepe the peace here, ho.

The D lines do not seem to have been selected and abridged from Q, but to be a different and an older version and are not without interest in and for themselves. To regard the D scene as a corruption of the scene from *2 Henry IV* is simply absurd. It is not corrupt, it is different and is manifestly revised into the form in which it appears in *2 Henry IV*.

Exactly the same relation between the two texts appears at the opening of *2 Henry IV*. There is no Induction by Rumour in D, and Northumberland very naturally carries the burden of the ill news. It was his originally. Some of Northumberland's words from D are spoken by Rumour in 2 *Henry IV*, but for the most part the speeches are different. After the defeat at Shrewsbury, D has Northumberland enter "alone in his garden and night-cappe," saying, "Tis noys'd abroad that Harry Monmouth fell," etc. "Tis noys'd" has been changed in Q to "my [Rumour's] office is to noyse abroad." Northumberland's heart misgives him and he says:

> But yett my hart is dull, & slow beleife
> Takes but faint houldings,

and four lines further on he says,

> Oh I feare,
> My sad hart saies. Rebellion had ill lucke.

Further on (I, i, 130) Morton's account of the disastrous battle appears in shorter form, and we find in D "The feare gave wings to flight." There is so much of this excellent poetry special to D that one can hardly doubt that it is made up in part of hitherto unrecognized words of Shakespeare.

The end of 2 *Henry IV* when compared with D makes clear the whole relationship between what seems to be the original and the revision. After his excursions in Holinshed and Gloucestershire Shakespeare returns to the fundamental story. At the very end there are word-for-word parallels between D and 2 *Henry IV*. In IV, v, which deals with the stealing away of the crown by the Prince and with the final reconciliation of father and son, the agreement is close. Again in V, ii, 14–34, there is reproduced the uneasiness of the new King's brothers and their reassurance (44–61). After this passage D has twenty-four lines special to itself, ending, however, with ll. 141–45. At this point 2 *Henry IV* alone has the reconciliation of the King with the Chief Justice. Then in V, v. 44–74, comes the rejection of Falstaff, practically the same in the two versions except for the loss of two lines at the end, canceled by Sir Edward Dering from D, and for the fact that in l. 48 "Brother of Clarence" appears in D instead of "My Lord Chief Justice," the latter being a witness to the introduction of that functionary in Shakespeare's revision.

The characters in D are throughout an old and essential group; they differ somewhat from those in Q and F of *1* and *2 Henry IV*. Sir Edward Dering has made various changes to accommodate his special performance, but nevertheless it is easy to see that Westmoreland is a more prominent figure in Q than in D. Sir Walter Blunt takes Westmoreland's place in the first scene, and John of Lancaster farther on. The part of Prince John of Lancaster is fuller in D except that he has no military role. Sir John Blunt seems to have had a part in D. Gadshill is absent, and there is a confusion about his part in *The Famous Victories*. The names of Harvey and Rossell appear as in Q, and Rossell seems to be a name for Bardolf, whose part is in general more important in D than in Q. Peto plays but a small part in D, and Poins often takes his place. Indeed, Poins is relatively more important in D than in QF. Vernon does not appear in D; nor does the Archbishop of York.

In the parts of D corresponding to *2 Henry IV* the absences of characters are wholesale. Attention has already been called to the fact that D has no trace of Justice Shallow or any of his entourage, no mention of or allusion to Pistol or Doll, and of the Chief Justice, whose relations to the Prince and to Falstaff are most important features of *2 Henry IV*, there is only an official trace.

Almost the entire plot of *1 Henry IV* is included in D, although there are a good many brief passages in the standard texts not present, as well as several longer passages that do not appear. Of the longer passages the first is the whole of II, i— Gadshill, the Ostler, and the Carriers in the innyard at Rochester. It is worth noting that Gadshill's role is confused in D and clear in QF. The next long passage not in D is the episode of the Welsh ladies in III, i, 192–272, which adds nothing essential to the plot and may well be revisional. The same is true of the comments of the Prince and Westmoreland on Falstaff's soldiers (IV, ii, 53–86). The last passage of any length to be absent from

D is IV, iv, the dialogue between the Archbishop of York and Sir Michael. It is not necessary to the story of Hotspur's defeat at Shrewsbury, but does have a bearing on the serious plot of Part II, and is therefore probably revisional. The hypothesis examined here is that D is in contents a complete play, on the original theme, and that this passage has no bearing on the original theme, although the scene may be anticipatory of the expansions in the revision of Part II.

The parts of D that correspond to 2 *Henry IV* are relatively small in number, but they carry through to the end the story of the wild life of Prince Hal, his reformation, the Percy rebellion, the death of the king, and the rejection of Falstaff. They contain not a single word that does not bear on the story, except the one rather simple scene between Falstaff and Mrs. Quickly. Compared with the whole of the rich play of 2 *Henry IV* they seem extremely bare, but if one remembers that they are *ex hypothetesi* the finishing of a play, they are in every way adequate. It is hard to believe that anybody could or would have cut down by selection 2 *Henry IV* in this fashion, but, in the light of what Shakespeare did, it is easy to see that by adding (from unused parts of Holinshed's *Chronicle*) the deception and defeat of the rebels who were still in the field, and by introducing a wealth of new comic characters, it was possible to expand it into a great drama in two parts. Shakespeare did this by amplifying less than one-third of the original *Henry IV* play into a drama of nearly 3,500 lines.

D is consistent within itself both in content and in style. Even the version of the comic scene (II, 1) is merely a commonplace squabble between Falstaff and the Hostess at the Boar's Head tavern, where the fat knight's pocket has been picked. It is different in kind of comicality from the brilliant and more sensational version of the scene in its revised form, and widely different from the other comic scenes in 2 *Henry IV*, which have a zest and variety of life and character unknown to this little scene in D and to comic scenes in *1 Henry IV*.

Part II is different too in its dramaturgy. In writing his new play Shakespeare rebuilt the whole structure. The impact of Hotspur's overthrow was plainly on Northumberland, always an important man in Shakespeare's eyes, and Shakespeare develops this idea. He imagines Northumberland awaiting with guilty conscience the news of the battle—early cheerful rumor swept away by disastrous truth. Shakespeare (with Virgil's help) invented the figure of Rumour—and put much, not all, of the old material into Rumour's mouth.[34] The scene in D is a naturalistic dialogue between Northumberland and Morton. There was not a man alive who could have reconstructed such a scene from the Induction and the first scene of 2 Henry IV. The additions to Part II, which have been thought of as omissions, are inordinate in number. As complete omissions they are incredible, as additions they are magnificent. They may be described as all that pertains to the comic characters enumerated earlier in this chapter and all that pertains to Scroop, Archbishop of York, Lords Mowbray, Hastings and Bardolf, Sir John Coleville, and Prince John of Lancaster in his campaign against the rebels.

Moreover, if the present hypothesis is true, not only does it throw new light on the genesis of Shakespeare's two great plays, but it puts us in possession of a good many clever and even eloquent words and speeches we have not hitherto recognized as Shakespeare's.

CHAPTER 2

SOME EFFECTS OF ERRONEOUS
OR IMPERFECT THEORIES

IN the preceding chapter there is a brief account of the logical principles of classification as applied to Elizabethan dramatic texts with studies of certain Shakespearean quartos about whose definition errors have sometimes been made on a simple level of misunderstanding; namely, the use of impure contexts of abstraction. There is also an important group of texts whose misclassification has been due not primarily to faulty observation, but to false theory. There is a distinction in source of error but no great difference in unfortunate results. In Chapter 1 it was stated that the closest possible reconstruction of Shakespeare's original text depends immediately on correct definition of the early versions of his plays from which the determination must be made, and it was said that no *ad hoc* contrivance could be admitted.

When the course of inductive reasoning is interrupted before completion by the intrusion of a false or premature hypothesis, the nature of the mental process is changed from induction, or the observation and collection of data, to *a priori* or deductive reasoning; the search for truth ceases and argument begins. The truth having been supposedly established, the scholar concerns himself with fitting phenomena into place, merely seeks to prove that such and such an object belongs or does not belong to such and such an unshakably established class. In so doing he functions as an advocate and not as a scholar. Moreover, he tries to make fictitious classes include as many things as possible. For example, the theory of memorial reconstruction, for which there is neither evidence nor necessity, has become in the minds of some

Shakespeare scholars an established truth, so that they feel the want of this theory when it does not appear in textual studies.[1] It must also be said that positivism breeds intolerance. It is to this deductive and erroneous element in the classification of a number of Shakespearean texts that we shall devote this chapter.

Romeo and Juliet[2]

The textual history of Romeo and Juliet presents typical features. (1) There is a first quarto (1597), a shortened stage version that has been acted in the provinces. It shows actors' modifications and corruptions, although the corruptions are by no means so great as recent scholars, anxious to establish a priori theories, have represented them to be. This is partly due to the fact that the first quarto was derived from the earliest known version of the play and not from either of the two later versions —the second quarto and the folio. (2) The second quarto (1599) was printed from the foul papers of Shakespeare's revision, not of the first quarto as it stands, but from the original as yet uncorrupted form of the play before it went on the road. (3) The folio version (1623) was set up from the fair copy of Shakespeare's revision, which was the authorized playbook of the Lord Chamberlain's company. All three of these customary or necessary operations are denied by many modern scholars and editors, and since the nature and interrelations of the early texts are not understood, there is no certainty in the determination of the text of Romeo and Juliet.[3] Every such text will of course have variorum features, but it is necessary to see what the variants are.

There can be no reasonable doubt that the original of Q1 was taken on the road. There is evidence from two independent sources: the statement on the title page of Q1 and the records of the Lord Chamberlain's men while they were on tour.[4] The title page reads: "An excellent conceited Tragedie of Romeo and Iuliet. As it hath been often (with great applause) plaid publiquely, by the right Honourable the L. of Hunsdon his Seruants. London, Printed by Iohn Danter." This evidence is further strengthened by the fact that both the stage directions and the text indicate that Q1 has been prepared for performance by a smaller company. (Road companies were, of course, smaller than city companies.) It is also generally accorded that the plays of traveling companies, so far as known, were abridged from longer originals, and Q1 is, as compared with Q2, a shortened text. This shorter text appeared in print soon after the return of the Lord Chamberlain's company to their regular playhouses in London, when, presumably, such a shortened and adapted stage version (somewhat the worse for wear) would no longer be needed. It would have come into that class of derelict or unneeded texts from which a large number of Elizabethan printed plays were derived.[5] We have no proof of this, but it is certain that Q1 has the marks and features of such a play and that Danter was printing it before the death of the Earl of Cobham on March 5, 1597, since after that date the players were no longer Lord Hunsdon's men.

But in the matter of abridgment we are on firmer ground, and it is possible to show with at least reasonable probability that the text of Q1 has been shortened from a longer text. Furthermore, as indicated above, although there is no absolute certainty, it would be overmeticulous to deny that such shortening of plays for provincial, and perhaps other, performances was customary and no doubt necessary. It is possible to make out a very good case for the abridgment of a longer text of *Romeo and Juliet* into the dimensions of Q1 and to show that the work was intelligently carried out. The play, as we have seen, needed to be adapted for acting by a smaller company, but the prevailing motive seems to have been the shortening of the play as an end in itself. In general it may be said that one of the purposes of abridgment is to accelerate and sharpen the action, and this result is no doubt produced; but the motive in the case before us would probably be to preserve the interest of the drama in spite of the losses it was about to suffer. The test of the operation as a conscious process and not a mere degenerative series of omissions is to discover, if possible, evidences of judgment and skill in the cutting of lines and speeches according to the requirements of the plot. One might, for example, expect to find sacrificed a good deal of the interest of the play in the prevailing preference of the abridger for action as against characterization; also that such a person would excise repetitions, even when artistically effective, and would often let action speak for itself. To a certain extent this is true of the first quarto of *Romeo and Juliet*; one encounters prevailingly clear-cut omissions, leaving the two quarto texts (except for slight adaptations) pretty much alike in their undisturbed parts. But there is also a good deal of actual difference, cases in which it is not possible to say that such and such lines have been cut. These textual differences between Q1 and Q2, not merely shortenings of the latter, complicate the problem, which is no longer the mere abridgment of the longer text into the shorter one.

Let us first take examples of clear-cut abridgment. At the opening of the play, I, i, 71–88, together with some stage directions, go out and are replaced in Q1 by one long stage direction in which a street fight is provided for and left to convey its own meaning: "They draw, to them enters Tybalt, they fight, to them the Prince, old Mountague, and his wife, old Capulet and his wife, and other Citizens and part them." This is a clever and natural way of shortening the play. A good deal of blustering talk is left out, the Prince's speech is shortened by eight lines, and it is possible to dispense with eight of Benvolio's narrative lines, since the audience has just beheld what has happened, the two lines that are left him being sufficient for continuity. There are several other such substitutions of action for dialogue.

At the opening of the next scene (I, ii), Q1 omits three lines from the beginning of Capulet's speech. The gain is small, but the lines are unnecessary, and the aggregate of short omissions is considerable, as, for example, in the same scene where Capulet loses two lines in two different places (14–15, 18–19). The Nurse's garrulous repetition (ll. 53–57) goes, and Lady Capulet herself loses ll. 69–73 and 79–94, mostly in praise of Paris, and the lines are dispensable. It reveals care in abridgment to observe that the Nurse's l. 90, which depends on the long omission, is also absent from Q1. I, iv, loses twelve lines (17–28) of the wit combat between Romeo and Mercutio. The balcony scene offers a masterpiece of skillful cutting, and Cummings suggests that there is a tendency throughout Q1 to lighten the part of Juliet. But whatever the motive, we again have shortening of Juliet's part with the omission of ll. 121–36. It results in the running together of two of Juliet's speeches and is a real feat of abridgment, the cut being scarcely noticeable. An almost equally unobtrusive omission appears in ll. 149–55, where one can hardly tell that Romeo's speech is not an immediate reply to Juliet's shortened speech before. Another neat cut appears in the omission of five lines (9–14) from Friar Lawrence's soliloquy in the opening of scene iii. Their absence is not felt. This kind of abridgment continues throughout Q1.

A certain vagueness about the number of extras or mutes will be noted in the stage directions of the second quarto of *Romeo and Juliet*, a vagueness suggestive of relative abundance; whereas in the stage directions of Q1 the number of these subordinates is definite and closely restricted, as if the number available were small. For example, in Q2 the opening direction at IV, ii, reads "Enter Father Capulet, Mother, Nurse, and Serving men, two or three," and in Q1 "Enter olde Capolet, his Wife, Nurse, and Seruingman"; and again at the opening of I, iv, Q2 reads "Enter Romeo, Mercutio, Benvolio, with five or sixe other Maskers, torchbearers," and Q1 "Enter Maskers with Romeo and a Page." The Page is necessary, and the Maskers seem to be only Romeo, Mercutio, and Benvolio, who are the speakers. There are thus eight or nine actors provided for in Q2 and only four in Q1. To be sure, this is the only stage direction for the entrance of characters that Q1 gives in this scene, although there are needed not only the four provided for, but also Capulet, an old friend of his, Juliet, the Nurse, and the two Capulets to be identified by the Nurse at Juliet's request (the son and heir of old Tiberio and the County Paris). This would make a total of ten, but there is nevertheless a saving in Q1 of five or six maskers and an unknown number of torchbearers.

V, i, requires only three speaking characters, but V, ii, again taxes the resources of the Q1 company. In this act the assignment of speeches and parts is somewhat confused in Q2, but clear enough in Q1. Peter speaks for Balthazar in Q2. The greater clarity in Q1 may come about by a doubling, possibly by Kemp, in the parts of Peter and Balthazar. The italics in Q1 (iii, 70) of the stage direction *"They fight"* appear anomalously in Q2 in an unassigned line belonging originally to Paris's Page, *"O Lord they fight, I will go call the Watch."* It is clear that substituting a stage direction for the speech in Q1 would set an actor free, although to arrive at the Q2 text one would have to believe that in the manuscript of Q2 there was both a stage direction and a one-line speech. After the death of Juliet the stage fills up, and we may test the capacity of the Q1 company by the needs of that assemblage. Romeo, Juliet, and Paris lie slain. Balthazar, Paris's Page, and Friar Lawrence are brought in by the Watch. The Prince, Capulet and his lady, and Montague enter. This amounts to ten speaking characters, and that is apparently the limit of the touring company's capacity. The Watch in Q1 would be made up of extras. In Q2 three watchmen speak, but in Q1 the Watch has apparently only two members, and the speeches, except those of the Captain of the Watch, are extremely brief. There are inconsistencies and obscurities in stage directions in both quartos, but the intentional abbreviation of Q1 finds further confirmation. For example Montague, after saying that his wife is dead, adds "And yong Benuolio is deceased too," an uncalled-for change that certainly suggests scarcity of actors. Cummings makes it clear that there was no music in Q1.

Further evidences of abridgment appear in IV, i, 52–60 and 99–104. In neither instance is the omitted matter dramatically necessary, and neither omission causes confusion in the Q1 text. Friar Lawrence's long speech is cut at ll. 106–12, and this again disposes of a case of two versions of the same passage in Q2. At the end of his speech, ll. 113–20 are reduced to two, which are, however, adequate for the action of the scene. All in all, the Friar's description is cut from thirty-three to fourteen lines. The scene in Q1 ends in a perplexing way, and the situation is further complicated by the fact that the following scene (IV, ii) is so different in the two quartos that it is very hard to form any standard of comparison. The cutting of scene iii is, however, intelligible after the first part of Juliet's speech before she takes the potion. This speech suffers considerably in Q1, but is perhaps adequate. Five lines (15–19) go out, and Juliet addresses the vial, but the omitted lines are replaced by an appealing new line: "Ah, I doo take a fearfull thing in hand." Ll. 24–28 are replaced in Q1, strangely enough, by two and one-half lines based on the five deleted lines. The effect is good, and there is again the suggestion that Q1 may be based on a version other than Q2. The potion soliloquy suffers a cut of seventeen lines (34–50), and there is no trace of them in Q1. There are many such outright omissions in Q1, but we have yet to learn why paraphrases or differing lines appear in some scenes and not in others. An example of a mere paraphrase (there are not so many of this kind as has been thought) occurs in Juliet's soliloquy. One line, "Ah then I feare I shall be lunaticke," takes the place of seventeen appealing but incoherent lines. IV, iv, is difficult to analyze from the point of view of abridgment, and Cummings's discovery of an indication that Will Kemp may have been in the touring company may help to account for the state of the Q1 text. Instead of the Q2 "Call Peter," Q1 has "Will will tell thee where thou shalt fetch them."

In the last scene of the play Paris's opening speech and his Page's response have been shortened, but with certain not easily explained differences, and the same is true of Romeo's first speech. Ll. 50–53 reveal an omission that can be justified, since the remaining text from Q2 ("This is that banisht haughtie Mountague, / That murdered my loues cosen") is sufficient to account for Paris's hostility. Romeo's fine lines, 60–61 and 66–67, are cut as possibly unnecessary. It is noteworthy that Romeo's last speech (forty-seven lines) is left standing and in very good form. There was obviously a tendency in the abridgment to cut long speeches, but the intelligence of the abridger seems to have spared this one. He did, however, remove ll. 80–83, possibly because they were less necessary. An omission scarcely noticeable in Q1 was made from the first half of l. 91 to the last half of l. 101, the broken lines coalescing. But the poetic loss is considerable, however much we may admire the skill with which the cut is made. The passage at ll. 108–16 has certainly been shortened and is possibly corrupt, although Q1 is entirely coherent. Balthazar's speech (137–39) is cut for what seems to be a sufficient reason; namely, that the spectators had seen him asleep. Finally, we leave this summary of differences between the two texts with the puzzling observation that Juliet's lines on her farewell kiss (164–68) are omitted from Q1. Her other lines are relatively accurate reproductions of Q2. One can think of no reason for this omission except the speculative one that her part has elsewhere been reduced, or, indeed, that these lines were not present in the version from which Q1 was made.

It is customary to declare that the end of the play in Q1 is jumbled and a mere hodgepodge, but I fail to see why this opinion should be so positively held. Q1 seems to present the same original version as that of Q2, and at the end of the play follows Q2 with fair fidelity and is of almost equal length. Like many other parts of Q1, indeed throughout that text, the Q1 ending shows just those textual degenerations that were undergone to a greater or lesser extent by all plays acted by Elizabethan players. There is no argument to be constructed on the score of such textual degenerations, which are simply there, and no need of ambitious speculations to account for them. Such alterations, for reasons already stated, must have been recorded in prompt-books, else we should have had no record of them.[6]

Discounting the cuts that seem to have been made in Q2, the two quartos are certainly much alike, and yet there are textual differences that tend to fall into groups in certain places. If allowance is made in Q1 for the textual degeneration undergone by plays on the stage, for differences in spelling, and for scribal and printing variants, the versions of the two quartos may be described for large parts of the play as one and the same. And yet, as we have observed in passing, there are differences in various places not to be readily accounted for on the mere supposition that Q1 was cut down in length from Q2. It is moreover very difficult to see how Q2 as it stands could have been available for use in the shortening process. Q2 has been regarded on very good grounds as printed from Shakespeare's foul papers. But since the title page of Q2 states that it has been "newly corrected, augmented, and amended," a statement that there is no reason to distrust, Q2 seems to be Shakespeare's foul papers of a revision and not of an original. The normal process would have been for Shakespeare to revise an original and licensed manuscript of *Romeo and Juliet* and thus render it unfit for use in the theater and for resubmission to the censor. It has been argued that the careful statement on the title page is there merely as an advertisement of the publication and a declaration of the superiority of this quarto over the one published in 1597, but I can see no grounds for such an interpretation. Q2 bears few marks of the prompter's hand. The customary procedure would have been to have a manuscript after revision copied for the purposes of the theater and for it to become the company's authorized copy. Meantime, the revised manuscript, having been copied, would have become supernumerary and, as in the case of the second quarto of *Hamlet*, would seem to have fallen by gift, purchase, or otherwise into the printer's hands. In my opinion, this is exactly what happened with the second quarto of *Romeo and Juliet*. I therefore believe we may safely say that the original manuscript behind Q2 was Shakespeare's foul papers of a revision.

There are, however, two matters that seem to point to a special condition. The first of these is Mercutio's famous speech about Queen Mab (I, iv, 52–91). In Q2 nearly all of this speech, although written in blank verse, is set as prose, a circumstance that would suggest that the speech was revisional and had been added in prose form to the original text before it was revised into the form of Q2. Presumably a transcriber of playhouse copy would write it out as verse, and Q1 so prints it. The verse in Q1 is correct enough and goes wrong only in the line that makes a juncture with the text of Q2.

The other textual peculiarity of Q2 that possibly carries over into Q1 is the strange appearance of italic type in some of the speeches of the Nurse (I, iii, 2–78). This italic type in Q2 has attracted attention, and the current explanation is that in this scene the printer of Q2, possibly finding himself confronted with a damaged manuscript, seized upon a copy of Q1 and set up his text from it. This leaves an important question unanswered; namely, how did the italic type get into Q1? In my judgment, the best answer that has been advanced is that a portion of the Nurse's part was originally written in the Italian hand and that this was used in the composition of the play, being stupidly copied into the playbook in the Italian hand because it had been so written. The Italian script must have been a feature of the play before the correction, augmentation, and amendment announced on the title page of Q2 were carried out. The Nurse's part is a brilliant piece of comic writing, and if there was a revision, it is, with its expert characterization of the Nurse, just the sort of amplification one might expect. The Nurse's lines may have been written out in the Italian hand and actually uttered on the stage before they were copied into the prompt-book. There is nothing preposterous about this hypothesis, and something of the sort must have been done to get those italic lines into any playbook whatsoever. I therefore suggest that the Nurse's italic lines made their first appearance, possibly by revisional process, in the manuscript from which Q1 was abridged and later Q2 was printed. Once there in that form, the copy-following habits of certain, or perhaps all, Elizabethan scriveners would keep them as they were, and to an Elizabethan printer the Italian hand would call for italic type.

Admirable bibliographical shrewdness has been employed to interpret printing and textual data to show that Q1 was the source of the italic type and not Q2; but the data should be looked at from an exactly opposite direction. Q1 presents a correct version of the lines in question (why should it not, since Italian script was clearer than secretary?). There is, however, a further circumstance that confirms the proposed relation. The knife of the abridger was not idle in Q1. This passage is about ten prose lines shorter in Q1 than in Q2. If the compositor of Q2 laid aside his manuscript and resorted to the printed text of Q1, where did he get these omitted lines?

> *Old La:* Inough of this, I pray thee hold thy peace.
> Nurse: *Yes, Madam, yet I cannot chuse but laugh, to thinke it should leaue crying, and say I: and yet I warrant it had vpon it brow, a bump as big as a young Cockrels stone: a perillous knock, and it cryed bitterly. Yea quoth my husband, fallst vpon thy face, thou wilt fall backward when thou commest to age: wilt thou not* Iule? *It stinted, and said I.*

If the lines are an addition to Q2, why did the printer put them in italic type? They have been characteristically excised in Q1, yet they belong to original composition; for they present the very climax of the Nurse's vulgarity that wrings from Juliet the protest "And stint thou too, I prethee Nurse, say I." It seems tedious to argue that the suppositorily illegible manuscript of Q2 was suppositorily legible at that particular place.

The idea that the text of which Q1 is a shortened version was a different play from that appearing in Q2 receives support from an examination of the so-called un-Shakespearean passages in Q1. Among these the almost totally different version of II, vi, is significant. The scene in Q1 reads:

> See where she comes,
> So light of foote nere hurts the troden flower:
> Of loue and ioy, see see the soueraigne power.
>   *Iul: Romeo.*
>   *Rom:* My *Iuliet* welcome. As doo waking eyes
> (Cloasd in Nights mysts) attend the frolicke Day,
> So *Romeo* hath expected *Iuliet,*
> And thou art come.
>   *Iul:* I am (if I be Day)
> Come to my Sunne: shine foorth, and make me faire.
>   *Rom:* All beauteous fairnes dwelleth in thine eyes.

> *Iul*: *Romeo* from thine all brightnes doth arise.
> *Fr*: Come wantons, come, the stealing houres do passe
> Defer imbracements till some fitter time,
> Part for a while, you shall not be alone,
> Till holy Church haue ioynd ye both in one.
> *Rom*: Lead holy Father, all delay seemes long.
> *Iul*: Make hast, make hast, this lingring doth vs wrong.
> *Fr*: O, soft and fair makes sweetest worke they say
> Hast is a common hindrer in crosse way.

These lines can hardly be ascribed to any mere botching process. They have been admired by many scholars and with reason, but it is not so much a matter of excellence as of difference. The friar has command in Q2; whereas the talk of the lovers is freer and more ardent in Q1, a difference that motivates the two lines in which the passages come together:

> Part for a while, you shall not be alone,
> Till holy Church have ioynd ye both in one.

Another example of strikingly different versions is III, ii, 57–60, where Q2 reads:

> O break my hart, poore banckroute break at once,
> To prison eyes, nere look on libertie.
> Vile earth too earth resigne, end motion here.
> And thou and *Romeo* presse on heauie beare.

Q1 has,

> Ah *Romeo*, *Romeo*, what disaster hap
> Hath severd thee from thy true *Juliet*?
> Ah why should Heauen so much conspire with Woe,
> Or Fate enuie our happie Marriage,
> So soone to sunder vs by timeless Death?

There is no comparison between the passages, and the best that can be said in favor of Q1 is that it is a simple utterance on the subject of impending death and that it may be the ruins of a better passage.

Similarly, IV, v, 43–64, in Q2 are represented by a quite different passage in Q1. And yet the differences do not tell the whole story; for Q1 has in it many excellent and, one would think Shakespearean, lines and expressions that are not in Q2. The additional lines in Mercutio's dying speech (III, i, 99–114), though relatively crude, cannot perhaps be disposed of as mere actor's improvisation:

> A poxe of your houses, I shall be fairely mounted upon foure
> mens shoulders: For your house of the *Mountagues* and the
> *Capolets*: and then some peasantly rogue, some Sexton, some
> base slave shall write my Epitaph, that Tybalt came and broke
> the Princes Lawes, and *Mercutio* was slaine for the first and
> second cause. Wher's the Surgeon?
>   *Boy.* Hee's come sir.
>   *Mer.* Now heele keepe a mumbling in my guts on the
> other side, come *Benuolio,* lend me thy hand: a poxe of your
> houses.

Benvolio's two lines (I, iv, 7–8) in Q1 have commended themselves to editors:

> Nor no withoutbooke Prologue faintly spoke
> After the Prompter, for our entrance.

And there are other passages special to Q1 which can hardly be disposed of on the vague ground that they are un-Shakespearean.

The Merry Wives of Windsor[7]

The title page of the 1602 quarto of *The Merry Wives of Windsor* tells us that the play is by Shakespeare and that it has been acted before the Queen "and elsewhere." The inference is that the play in this form has been on the road and that Shakespeare's company, the Lord Chamberlain's servants, have acted it in the provinces.

The rival text is that of the First Folio of 1623, a clean and readable text carefully divided into acts and scenes, but full of errors, misreadings of manuscript, and omissions. Certain peculiarities of scribal style in the play make it clear that the folio version was printed from a scrivener's copy and not from a playhouse manuscript. The characters appearing in each scene are

listed at the beginning of the scene and not, as is the usual practice, at the points in the dialogue where the characters enter.
Exits are also not distributed, but are lumped together with an
"Exeunt" at the end of each scene. With one minor exception
there are no stage directions. It follows from these and other
indications that the text of the folio cannot have been set up from
a theatrical copy. This supposition is rendered more secure by
another observation. The first five plays of the First Folio were
printed from specially prepared manuscripts. After the delivery
of these manuscripts, Heminge and Condell, possibly finding the
copying of plays too expensive, sent other sorts of copy to the
printers; ultimately many of their own playbooks. If therefore
the folio text of *The Merry Wives of Windsor* was set from a
transcript, of what was it a copy? Presumably it was a reproduction of the company's playbook or "original," and this conjecture
introduces many uncertainties into the determination of the folio
text. The scrivener himself may have misread his document and
made errors, omissions, and changes. The playbook before being
copied may have served as a prompt copy and have undergone
the various changes, adaptations, and degenerations suffered inevitably by any Elizabethan play that was acted on the stage.
The best one can do is to accept the folio text as having behind it
the full-length play that Shakespeare wrote. Indeed, one can be
fairly sure that this much at least is true, for although the quarto
is a shortened version of the original, it nevertheless supplies
missing parts, ranging from single words and lines to considerable
passages; it itself becomes a witness for the validity of the folio.
The folio, however, is shaky as an authority and imperfect; in
fact, in so far as the texts cover the same ground, often inferior
to the much despised quarto of 1602.

Ever since A. W. Pollard classified the 1602 quarto as a
"bad" quarto, editors and commentators have heaped abuse upon
it, sometimes to show that it was actually a *bad* quarto and more
frequently to use its putative badness to bolster up a theory of
its piratical or mnemonic origin. In reality, the quarto text, apart
from its being an abbreviated stage version of the original so

altered as to dispense with several actors, is not a bad quarto at all, and no one seeing certain merits in the 1602 quarto need feel disgraced by defending a document about which so many disagreeable things have been said. It is necessary in the cause of truth to examine the quarto and compare it with the folio in order to see just how good or how bad the quarto text is. It is also necessary to show that the quarto is a stage version of such a kind as would be made by intelligent actors and is thus a normal product of the time.

There is one happy circumstance that we shall find of great advantage. We know from the discoveries of Leslie Hotson, confirmed by those of William Bracy, that *The Merry Wives of Windsor* was not only acted but written in the spring of 1597. This discovery makes use of the tradition that Shakespeare wrote the play in response to a command by the Queen, who wished with characteristic frivolity to see Falstaff in love. Records and circumstances seem to point to the Garter Feast at the palace of Westminster on April 23, 1597, and the installation ceremonies at Windsor on May 24 of that year.

Another circumstance of the period following the spring of 1597 offers a plausible occasion for the preparation of the quarto text, which, as said above, is certainly a stage version. Pembroke's men gave great offense by their performance of Nashe's *The Isle of Dogs* at the Swan in the summer of 1597, which resulted in an attack by the Privy Council not only on Nashe and other offenders, but on all theaters and stage plays. The theaters at Shoreditch and on the Bankside were ordered dismantled, and all dramatic activity was commanded to cease. A result of this disaster was that in August and September 1597 the Lord Chamberlain's men made a tour of the provinces. On such a tour it would have been natural for them to take with them this new and doubtless popular play. They would probably have needed to shorten it, and since not all the actors would have gone on tour, to adapt it to a smaller troupe. These adjustments were apparently made and well made. The play belonged to the Lord Chamberlain's company, and they themselves went on this tour and were no doubt concerned with the play's success. There would have been no occasion for dishonesty. Indeed, the company would have used its best talent in the preparation of the stage version. These conjectures are natural and plausible. If they are correct, we have only the task of assessing the value and state of the quarto. This we shall do in the answering of two questions.

(1) Is the state of the quarto text such that its shortcomings could not have been produced by at least one extended tour of the provinces—and possibly further revivals on the stage between 1597 and 1602—and later by passing through the hands of a London printer? The answer is that such an experience could have produced such results, indeed that the quarto came out pretty well, since it maintained its integrity as a play and preserved astonishingly well a great deal of Shakespeare's original language and dramaturgy.

(2) How do we know that the quarto is a version shortened for acting and adapted to the needs of a different company? There is no brief or easy answer to this question, which cannot be settled except by much careful work, but we find in William Bracy's monograph precisely what we are looking for. We cannot repeat all of his findings, but we can make selections in order to rediscover and reassert the truth as it is embodied in an actual document.

One may believe that in the Lord Chamberlain's company in 1597, a time when Shakespeare himself was in his busiest period of dramatic activity, a sound and skillful job of adaptation would have been done. In this case it would have been necessary to adjust such a play to the company and the stage—prompter's markings and the casting of characters. The title page of the quarto says that the play, apparently that very copy, had been performed before her Majesty, and adds "and elsewhere," which suggests performances in the country. The stage version of *The Merry Wives* may thus have been prepared for acting at court and subsequently carried on the road. The reason for making this proviso is that in some matters the quarto seems to be an older version of the play than that contained in the folio. Bracy thinks that the adaptations to staging and the shortening were carried through as one process and by a person or persons very familiar with the play. Little, one may say almost nothing, of dramatic significance was omitted from the abbreviated version, although the compression often involves not only the shortening of speeches but the omission or subordination of characters. The hand of the prompter is clearly to be seen. Stage business is skillful and in a number of cases takes the place of omitted matter. Several long stage directions seem not so much descriptive as necessary. Long speeches are continually reduced in length, but in all instances the parts left standing carry forward the dramatic action, and cues are not wantonly disturbed or changed. Abridgment or adaptation is not, however, limited to long speeches, and the shorter cuts are usually deftly made. Subject matter not connected with the action or of only slight interest suffers, and in the shorter cuts, of which there are many, excessive word-play, speech amplification, elaborate comparisons, and, it seems probable, certain topical references go out. At the beginning and the end of scenes there is much rephrasing and adjustment of lines apparently designed to hasten the opening of the dramatic action (in several places to get Falstaff on the stage more quickly) and to close the scene for what is about to follow. Main characters thus begin to speak sooner, the plot is clarified and the denouement is hastened. There are also fewer actors required in the quarto than in the folio in response, no doubt, to necessities in the casting of parts, there being no less than nineteen instances of characters omitted or, although still appearing in the old stage directions, robbed of their speeches. There are also some indications of the doubling of parts, and, finally, some whole scenes and quite long parts of scenes are cut. The stage directions in the quarto seem to be in part new and in part carried over from an original. Some of them, as suggested above, seem designed to serve the purpose of abridgment. For example, in the case of Bardolf in I, i, the quarto removes his lines with some reassignment and omits references to him, although his name still appears in a stage direction. The Boy in scene iii of the same act is retained in an entrance and an exit, but has no lines. This character is consistently removed from scenes ix and x in the quarto, although he has some importance and interest in the folio. Stage directions in the quarto, ll. 649 and 721, have apparently come over from the original manuscript.

Let us now take up some parts of the quarto in detail and refer the reader to Dr. Bracy's study for a complete account. We use the standard references to the acts, scenes, and lines of the folio version and, when necessary, scene and serial line numbers for the quarto.

I, i (F 289 ll.; Q 118 ll.).—In this scene the action of the two versions is the same, but Q is quicker in getting Falstaff on the stage. Sir Hugh's speech containing the "arbitarments" crux occurs earlier in Q than in F, but with entire fitness. It is a paraphrase of the F speech (which has "umpire"), and the change seems intentional and not anticipatory. In F Sir Hugh has only one line after Falstaff's entrance, and in Q there are two cuts, ll. 130–52 and 172–91, which eliminate Bardolf, although his listing in a stage direction indicates that he was in the original. Q l. 77 leaves only Slender and Anne on the stage. Simple, who has only three lines in F, does not appear in this scene. The only interest in the long cut (ll. 205–85) is in the characterization of Slender, but there is enough of such material left in Q to serve the purpose of showing him up as a simpleton. The variants in this scene in dialogue and diction are fairly numerous, but the essence of the scene is preserved. There are frequent correspondences in lines, and we begin already to see that Q is prevailingly derived from Shakespeare's original.

I, iii, (F 97 ll.; Q 103 ll.).—In this scene the correspondence in dialogue between Q and F is so close that a manuscript source for Q may be regarded as certain. At l. 25 (Q 159) in Nym's speech Q rather than F seems to preserve the original reading, since Nym's speech is linked with a preceding speech by Pistol. The F reading is possibly due to revision or actor-degeneration in this text. Also in the repartee about stealing, Q seems to preserve the original. Q ll. 184–88 (in verse) are a condensation of

F ll. 47–53 (in prose) and seem too good to attribute to the forgetfulness of a reporter. Rearrangements in Q (if they are such) seem in every case to be improvements. Q prints the whole scene in verse (except Falstaff's later speech), and F in prose (except one speech each of Falstaff and Pistol), and the inference from the greater use of prose in Q would be that Shakespeare's original manuscript had in it a great deal of verse (usually of an imperfect and hasty character). When one finds verse in Q and prose in F, the inference would be that F has been at least partly revised in prose. In the case in question, as well as in other cases, Q is closer to the original than F.

I, iv (F 154 ll.; Q 73 ll.).—In this scene two long cuts appear in Q, both apparently motivated by a desire to reduce the number of characters or to hasten the action. Ll. 1–15, the dialogue between Rugby and Mistress Quickly, are unnecessary to the action and are omitted, and it may be that this omission permits an actor from the previous scene to double as Rugby. The omission of ll. 141–80 removes Fenton from the scene. The theme of Fenton and Anne belongs to Act III in both versions, and Mistress Quickly, who converses with Fenton, is more prominent in F and would be less needed in Q. Q condenses the challenge of Dr. Caius and suffers somewhat in clarity, but is perhaps adequate. Almost no French phrases appear in the doctor's part in Q, and one might think that they have been cut as inappropriate for a provincial audience. There is no dramatic loss in this scene, although Fenton is omitted and Caius's part much reduced.

II, i (F 218 ll.; Q 155 ll.).—The dialogue between Mistress Page and Mistress Ford is shortened and rephrased, and two long speeches (ll. 46–70, 86–95) are omitted in Q, but there is no damage to the plot or situation. Shorter cuts are carefully made; for example, ll. 120–26, where Q begins and ends with lines from F, and ll. 132–41, where the speech in Q is skillfully condensed by the use of significant phrases from F. Everywhere it is usual to find that Q, although shorter, makes good sense and sticks closely to the F wording. In the last case an original F line linked with the next speech ends the Q cut. In every case cutting, transference of lines, and paraphrasing proceed in Q without loss of dramatic content and clarity. It is again obvious that such careful work could have been done only from a manuscript and that a mnemonic origin could hardly have produced such a result. The cutting here and elsewhere is so expert and the condensation so clear and economical that it seems perverse to regard it as anything except the intelligent shortening of a dramatic manuscript.

II, iii (F 89 ll.; Q 62 ll.).—Here Slender's name remains in a Q listing, but he has nothing to say in the scene. Again one sees, as in I, i, and in other places, cutting fairly obviously intended to shorten the play. The unimportant conversation between Caius and Rugby, for example, is shortened. There are two cuts (ll. 36–38, 43–58) in which Shallow's speeches in briefer form clearly bridge the omission and give the content of the repetitious seventeen-line passage in F. Similarly, several speeches in F (ll. 71–78) are condensed into one five-line speech in Q, which, however, contains a reference to Slender, his removal from the scene having been overlooked.

III, i (F 109 ll.; Q 80 ll.).—The cutting of Slender's part, which seems to be a tendency in Q, is still greater in the next scene, the only vestige of him being his appearance in a stage direction at Q l. 721. A reference to him in F (l. 32) has not been carried over into Q. The opening dialogue between Sir Hugh and Simple is much abridged, but with no loss of sense. From the entrance of the duelists and the Host (l. 36) the two texts correspond closely. The often described variant (ll. 107–8) in which Q (ll. 770–71) preserves the original "hand terrestrial . . . hand celestial" appears in this scene. F, which is in prose, has apparently suffered from scribal omission. At Q l. 775 Bardolf is addressed, although he is not on the stage. Bracy's suggestion is that one actor was doubling in the parts of Bardolf and Simple. Here again we have in this scene the omission of repetitious matter with the details of the plot left intact. This would seem to be a necessary scene for support of the pirate-actor theory, according to which the speeches of the host are superior to those of other characters, and his knowledge of other parts improves the text in general when he is present. The first statement is possibly true, although not necessarily significant, but the second is doubtful, since in many places in Q where the Host is not present the correspondence with F is as good or better. Incidentally, it might be remarked that immediately before the Host's entrance there is cutting and rephrasing, which one would not expect if the Host had been familiar with the text. The Host's excellence is not overpowering even in this scene. He was apparently a popular character, and the maker of the stage version seems to have treated his part with some liberality.

IV, ii (F 208 ll.; Q 92 ll.).—In this scene Q has been cut to about one-half the length of F. This has been done principally by shortening long speeches and by omitting details unnecessary to the plot. The speeches remaining in Q are carried over from F, or adequately combined, or rephrased, the language and sense remaining the same in both versions. It is a model of the adapter's skill. F ll. 59–66, the "kill-hole" speech and Mistress Ford's response, are cut. Ll. 86–107, in which Mistress Ford tells Mistress Page about Ford's abuse of Falstaff, are also cut. Ll. 110–50, directions to servants and their replies, are condensed and properly transferred to the beginning of the scene. Ll. 153–71, in which Ford searches the basket and is reproved by the company, are absent from Q, and one would expect a stage direction, but there is none. The remainder of the scene is omitted from Q, but dramatic continuity is not affected, and the action is greatly expedited. This scene is full of action, and it may be that stage business took the place of many lines. Such as are left are fairly faithful to the F text.

IV, iii (F 13 ll.; Q 12 ll.).—This scene deals with the obscure theme of the stolen horses. Shallow and Slender (with others) enter at the end of the scene, but have no part in the following one. There is no evidence of superiority in the Host's lines or in the scene. Certainly both texts have suffered in this area of the plot.

V, i–v.—Of these scenes ii, iii, and iv are absent from Q. They are, however, either repetitious or unnecessary. In scene i cutting is so drastic that one wonders if Q itself has been tampered with. In this scene Falstaff's first speech in F is taken over by Q, and the rest of the scene is cut. The cut is, however, justifiable, since it presents only an outworn third interview between Falstaff and "Brome," but it loses for Q some very good talk by Falstaff. This cut continues through Falstaff's first speech in scene v, which is represented by one line, but Falstaff comes back to the F version at l. 14. After this there are several cuts and condensations before the fairy episode begins. So much of Falstaff's best wit is not in Q that it is natural to suspect that F has been rewritten and amplified. The final scene in *The Merry Wives* seems to be of different composition in the two versions, although F and Q are united by some phrases, such as "middle earth . . . Welsh fairy" (ll. 84–85) and others. A long cut in Q removes references to Windsor, heraldry, and the Garter, and the reference to "the mad Prince of Wales" (Q ll. 1518–19) is not in F. There are, however, more resemblances after the fairies go out, although Fenton's speech (ll. 233–43) is cut in Q from eleven lines to two. The action in Q is in general agreement with F, but one can hardly see, after observing throughout the play the consistent work of the Q adapter, how he could have been working on a play that, in this scene, was like the present text of F. Pistol has lines in F that do not reappear in Q, and Mistress Quickly's four-accented trochaic lines in Q are widely different from the lines she speaks in F. These Q lines may be vestiges of an earlier form of the complete play. One cannot say that Q breaks down in the last scene, since it is, with slight exceptions, perfectly clear and characteristically direct. One can only say that, where both texts of the play are preserved, Q differs from F more widely at the end of the play than at any other place.

In view of all the uncertainty that surrounds the text of the First Folio and its history, this is as fair an account of the relation of the 1602 quarto of *The Merry Wives of Windsor* to the play as Shakespeare wrote it as can be made. One has to use F as a text of reference because there is no other way of guessing at the text of the original play. F, to be sure, is often supported as well as corrected by Q. Q, allowing for cuts and rearrangements, is simpler than F, and so far as it extends and escapes mutilation, it is possibly closer to Shakespeare's first version than is F.

We announced as the purpose of Bracy's textual study the intention of proving that the 1602 quarto of *The Merry Wives* began as a legitimate stage version of the play, and he seems to have proved that it was, and a very good one. But the quarto text cannot have had two or three different origins, and if it began as a normal, even skillful, version of a longer text, it cannot have come into existence in some other way as well. The experiences that it underwent when it was possibly on the provincial stage and when it was being printed were certainly harmful, but they have been exaggerated; for with proper corrections and in the light of its history the quarto text is both good and Shakespearean.

Hamlet[8]

The title page of the 1604–5 *Hamlet* (some copies were pre-dated by a year) reveals certain special features:

The Tragicall Historie of Hamlet, Prince of Denmarke. By William Shakespeare. Newly imprinted and enlarged to almost as much againe as it was, according to the true and perfect Coppie. At London, Printed by I. R. for N. L. and are to be sold at his shoppe vnder Saint Dunstons Church in Fleetstrete. 1604.

The claim "Newly imprinted and enlarged to almost as much againe as it was, according to the true and perfect Coppie," although not unique, certainly indicates revision before publication.[9] J. Dover Wilson's extensive studies of the special characteristics of Shakespeare's handwriting, leading to the errors to which its peculiarities gave rise, and also his conclusion that Shakespeare's punctuation was habitually light, rhetorical, and individual, have certainly advanced to a point of plausibility. In this he is greatly assisted by his conjecture that the quarto compositor was ignorant, but within limits faithful to his copy. Granted that the second quarto text as set up by the compositor and corrected by the proofreader was very full of errors, the fact remains that it is, as a whole, the text nearest to what Shakespeare wrote.

The problem that the second quarto presents is, moreover, far simpler than that presented by the folio of 1623. It seems probable enough and within the lines of customary procedure that a transcript or clean copy of the revised manuscript was made. The transcript would have been more accurate than is the printed quarto, and it is the subsequent career of that transcript after it came into the hands of the company that demands attention. The following is what I suggest must have happened. There is no reason to think that the clean copy of Shakespeare's manuscript was not at first a good one, but many changes were in store for it. The first of these, of course, would have been the extensive preparation of the transcript for the casting of parts and the use of the prompter. The formal work has been well done, and the stage directions have certainly had professional treatment. This early operation would only have been a beginning; for the playhouse manuscript would have been subject to other modifications as often as it was revived or even played. It is a mistake to lump these successive changes together as one operation and to attribute them to a single scribe and to designate that scribe by a single letter of the alphabet. No doubt the greater number of changes would have been made when the full text of *Hamlet* was put on the stage; but it must be remembered that this performance was only the first of we do not know how many stagings, each of which would have demanded its quota of alterations to suit the company performing it and their ideas of who should speak the lines and how they should be spoken. We are forced to conclude that Shakespeare's original manuscript of his revision, the one from which the clean copy had been made, was no longer needed, and that for any one of the variety of reasons already suggested or for reasons as yet unknown, it was turned over to the printers and issued as the *Hamlet* of 1605.[10] As explained above, wear on the stage has affected all plays—in Elizabethan times, long before, and ever since. It was also suggested above that the many changes made in the staging of a play would have to be recorded in the prompt-book; for that was the instrument by means of which the play was performed. Whether an actor varied from the original text because he chose to, or because he could not do otherwise, would in either case have to be a matter of record.

The occasion for these remarks is what seems to have happened to the clean copy of Shakespeare's play after it became the prompt-book at the Globe. As printed in the First Folio of 1623 the text certainly begins to show the widely present and ill-defined degeneration that seems to appear progressively in the texts of plays that were repeatedly acted on the stage. Expletives, vocatives, inversions, simplifications, and modernizations of language begin to appear. The English language was, as everybody knows, taking on colloquial forms between 1605 and 1623. The printers of the folio were modernist, so probably were the actors, although a good deal of the older language slips by them. The folio printers were actually revolutionary in the matter of punctuation, although, here again, they were not thorough in their reforms.

Dover Wilson concludes that the preparation for the staging of the *Hamlet* transcript was so skillfully done that Shakespeare must have been in some way responsible for it, and that in his original manuscript Shakespeare left certain cruxes and tangles that he later set right in the transcript. There seems no improbability in these suppositions, nor in the idea that the shortening of the play was also done with exceptional skill, sometimes so neatly as to suggest the hand of Shakespeare himself. We should also record our belief that the text of the First Folio was set up from a manuscript, and not from a printed quarto that had been corrected from a prompt-book; but we shall leave this matter for later consideration.

The first quarto of *Hamlet* (1603), now mistakenly regarded by many scholars as printed from a reported or pirated prompt-book of the Globe, shows resemblance not only to the text of the First Folio, a feature that would be easily explained if the current theory were true, but also to the text of the second quarto (1605). There can be no doubt about this resemblance; for the cases of textual agreement between Q1 and Q2 against F have been collected by Wilson and, without counting variants in stage directions, amount to the astonishing total of 163. Agreements the other way about—namely, between F and Q1 against Q2— amount to 168, which is but little more. In both series agreement is in large matters as well as small, striking differences as well as merely formal and incidental ones. To meet this difficulty and to save the theory that Q1 is a degenerate form of F some scholars have introduced an intervening process. The printer of Q2, they say, had at hand a copy of Q1 to which he resorted from time to time in search of guidance in the reading of Shakespeare's manuscript. The device has no testimony to support it and but little convincing bibliographical evidence. The conjecture makes use of the dangerous practice of introducing into a system an invented cause, and it does not strengthen the argument to point out that these unexpected Q1–Q2 parallels occur mainly in the first act of Q1. Wilson's collation shows that this is hardly true, and, as is common knowledge, Q1 gets worse as it goes on, and fewer parallels would be expected.

If, as I believe, Q2 and the transcript behind F rest on the same revised manuscript of Shakespeare's play, we note the puzzling fact that Q1 agrees sometimes with Q2 against F, and sometimes with F against Q2. Out of 78 major variants—those affecting the meaning of the text—in which Q1 and Q2 agree against F, there are 64 in which Q1 seems unquestionably to support Q2, and only 14 about which there can be the slightest doubt. Out of 66 major variants in which Q1 and F agree against Q2, there are 59 cases in which Q1 has the original reading and only 7 that might be open to question. These determinations are based on individual judgments and the opinions of editors, but I am by no means sure that the doubtful cases are not fewer than stated. When there are misreadings and printers' errors in Q2 and F is correct, Q1 ought to conform with the F reading, and when there are errors or stage alterations in F and Q2 has the original reading, Q1 ought to agree with Q2. Q1 follows just this pattern in an overwhelming number of cases. There is only one possible explanation of this phenomenon, and that is, that Q1 is a version of Shakespeare's original play and is not a reported version of either Q2 or F.

Certain well known facts confirm this view. At least one very striking structural difference between Q1 and the other texts has long been known, and one wonders whether scholars have not gone too far in their contempt for Q1.[11] In the standard texts Polonius plans to "loose my daughter to him," while he and the king, as "lawful espials," hide behind the arras in order to overhear the conversation between Hamlet and Ophelia and thus see if Hamlet will give away his secret. This is in II, ii. Hamlet appears reading, and Polonius makes his own test. Then Rosenkrantz and Guildenstern carry out in the same scene their interrogation of Hamlet. The Players appear (II, ii, 224–323), and in the beginning of the third act (III, i, 1–28) Rosenkrantz and Guildenstern report their failure. Finally, the story of the Ophelia test is resumed (III, i, 28–96). In Q1 the same series of events are very different in arrangement. Ophelia is absent from the beginning of II, ii, and enters first at II, ii, 40. In Q1 there is no gap between the making of the Polonius plot and its execution. The management of the standard versions is much better, but that is not the point. Hamlet enters at once after the plan has been stated, utters his soliloquy (badly garbled), beholds Ophelia, and the get-thee-to-a-nunnery scene ensues. Polonius's own test, that of Rosenkrantz and Guildenstern, and the arrival and first interview with the Players follow and do not precede Hamlet's soliloquy and his meeting with Ophelia. Moreover these scenes as presented in Q1 are organically joined with one another. It is very hard to see how a reporter (any variety of reporter) could or would in reproducing the Globe prompt-book have made such a change or, if he made it, have preserved so well the dramatic connections and continuity of Q1. The structure of Q1 has had reasonable defenders on the ground that it is more direct than the standard versions of the play and much quicker and clearer in action (which is not to say that the Q2-F arrangement is not superior, since it builds a broader and deeper suspense and increases the unity of the play by bringing in clearer motives). But the arrangement in Q1 carries this surprising evidence of its validity: it follows the source, and the standard version does not. It follows the arrangement of the German Hamlet, *Der bestrafte*

Brudermord, which we shall not at this time discuss, and has immediate support from the plot arrangement of Belleforest's *Histoires tragiques* and therefore of Saxo Grammaticus. In these sources the three attempts to discover Hamlet's secret are given in succession, as they are in Q1.

There is another considerable difference toward the end of the play, where the scenes are different and there are changes in motivation. Q1 does not have the scene (IV, vi) in which Horatio receives the letter from Hamlet about his adventures on the voyage, and there appears in Q1 an entirely different scene in which Horatio tells the Queen the story of Hamlet's escape. This scene, moreover, shows her clearly on Hamlet's side, as she is in Belleforest. Here, again, Q1 has too much originality and literary responsibility to be expected of any reporter.

The quarto of 1603 was certainly printed from a prompt-book that had had much use on the stage. We are told on the title page that it had been "diuerse times acted by his Highnesse seruants in the Cittie of London: as also in the two Vniversities of Cambridge and Oxford, and elsewhere." There is no reason to contest this statement, either in that the play had been acted by the King's company or in that it had been acted in the country; for these claims, which seem inconsistent with the theory that Q1 was taken down by stenography or pirated by one or more actors and sold to Nicholas Ling and John Trundle, seem to provide (prompter's markings excepted) for just such a document as we have before us. The natural inference is that when the traveling company, in this case the Lord Chamberlain's (later the King's) men, returned to London from tour, their prompt-book of *Hamlet* fell into the hands of the publishers.

To ascribe the various aberrations and peculiarities of the text of Q1 to a process of memorial reconstruction tells us very little, if anything; it merely substitutes a general unknown for particular difficulties. So varied was the experience of the stage version of *Hamlet* during its apparently long career on the provincial stage that it seems advisable to see whether the document itself will not tell its own story, although this is a harder and slower method to apply than a facile theory. If we accept the inferences from the title page and the evidences from comparison of texts as a working basis, we may believe that Q1 was a stage version of Shakespeare's *Hamlet* before a final revision. We may not arrive at conviction, but we shall at least be proceeding in a realistic way.

Our immediate question may be stated as whether or not the play of which Q1 is a prompt-copy was actually the standard version of *Hamlet* as we have it. A few precautionary inferences may be drawn. First, we may say that we can see no reason why members of the Lord Chamberlain's company going into the provinces and under the protection of the patron of that company should have been obliged to obtain dishonestly a copy of this play, or why they might not have taken a prompt-book with them. From the opinions here advanced we may believe that the corruptions of Q1 were due not to its origin, but to the alterations that the text suffered while it was a repertory play of a traveling company. From the state of the text we may infer that this company was both incompetent and inadequate in its personnel. Second, we may therefore be reasonably sure that the prompt-book underwent continual deterioration on the road and suffered more and more in its faithfulness to the original. This opinion may not be shared by those who doubt whether the forces at work on the prompt-book were strong enough to produce such a result, although I think it would be admitted that they were very great indeed. In other words, the particular evidence for this degeneration rests squarely on the belief that the prompt-book would have had to record the text as it could be and would be acted; otherwise the play could hardly have been revived as the company traveled from town to town. The various sorts of change in the prompt-book might thus be produced in the ordinary course of procedure of dramatic companies, especially when they were on tour, acting with diminished troupes and probably actors of poor quality. Else how are we to account for the rather large number of degenerate plays that have come down to us from Elizabethan times?[12]

The only feature that, so far as I am concerned, stands in the way of accepting the doctrine of a regularly descended prompt-book by process of continual change (usually, but not necessarily always, for the worse) is the matter of anticipations and recollections in the inferior texts; that is, cases in which various passages, short or long, written for a certain place in the action, appear either too soon or too late. The cause of such corruptions has been properly recognized as faulty memory and has driven students of Shakespeare and the Elizabethan drama to the conclusion that certain bad texts, among which is Q1, have been produced by a process, not well understood and having little evidence for its exclusive support, called memorial reconstruction. Stenography has been another frequent resort of Shakespeare students, as also the theory of a pirate actor stealing a play from his own company and selling it to a printer. The idea that I am advancing is that the Q1 text of *Hamlet* came into its present state in an ordinary way and that it is not necessary to make use of special hypotheses. On the whole, it seems better to view the matter in a more prosaic way and at least to see if ordinary practices would produce the conditions we find in this version of the play.

The problem of the versions of *Hamlet* is one of the oldest problems of Shakespearean criticism and has had continual attention from scholars for generations. There now emerges a plain tale of actuality that is worthy of credence and would be believed generally but for the intrusion of unnecessary theories that break the line of plain truth. The facts, which conform with custom, ought to be allowed to speak for themselves.

Q1 is a somewhat degenerated version of Shakespeare's earliest known play on the theme of Hamlet. Q2 was printed from the foul papers of Shakespeare's revision of that first *Hamlet*, probably from a better version than Q1 presents.[13] F began as a fair copy of Shakespeare's revision of his first version, that is, from the manuscript from which Q2 was printed. This does not say that there may not have been some alterations when the fair copy was made for submission to the censor and the use of the dramatic company. As the playbook of the King's men, this fair copy inevitably underwent changes in the theater. It finally served as copy for the printing of *Hamlet* in the First Folio of 1623.[14] This chapter adds a possibly unnoticed confirmation of the fact that Q1 was a version of Shakespeare's oldest play on Hamlet, since its text arbitrates between the texts of Q2 and F when they disagree.

Other Quartos in Dispute[15]

In Chapter 1 an attempt was made to show that the first quarto of *King Lear* and the 1609 quarto of *Pericles* cannot be included in the class of "bad" quartos or "reported" versions. In this chapter we have given reasons for rejecting from such categories the first quarto of *Romeo and Juliet,* the 1602 quarto of *The Merry Wives of Windsor,* and the first quarto of *Hamlet.* In these cases the ground of rejection was that the context of generalization or classification is impure, as the logicians say, mainly because it fails to give proper recognition to the alterations and degenerations wrought by use on the Elizabethan stage, which is a major factor, as shown in prompt-books both in manuscript and in print. There are also other Shakespearean quartos that should be considered.

The 1600 quarto of *Henry V* is almost unmarked, and seems not to have been printed from a prompt-book. Nothing therefore can be certainly determined about it in this connection, although it is at least possible that the quarto is based on an earlier version of *Henry V* than that of the folio of 1623.[16] H. T. Price regards the quarto as a stenographic version.

The quarto of *The First Part of the Contention betwixt the two famous Houses of Yorke and Lancaster* (1594) and that of *The true Tragedie of Richard Duke of Yorke* (1595) have been described as reported versions of *2* and *3 Henry VI* as they appear in folio, but this is certainly an error. The indications are that the quartos are derived from earlier versions of these plays revised by Shakespeare into the folio forms late in the 1590's. The problems posed by these quartos are, if one looks at the facts, very simple. These facts are more definitive than in any other of the texts so far examined. The problem presented by the quartos and the folio bears some resemblance to that of the first quarto and the later versions of *Hamlet* and *Romeo and Juliet,* since we again have early versions of two plays by Shakespeare that were also later put into more perfect forms.

That the *Contention* and the *True Tragedy* are plays by Shakespeare may be inferred with fair certainty from Robert Greene's attack on Shakespeare as "Shakescene" in *A Groatsworth of Wit* (1592),[17] entered in the Stationers' Register on September 20, 1592, seventeen days after Greene's death. It contains the parody of a line from the *True Tragedy* repeated in the folio of *3 Henry VI* (I, iv, 137):

> Oh Tygers hart wrapt in a womans hide.

Greene's line is "Tygers hart wrapt in a Players hyde." Therefore the *True Tragedy* must have been in existence before Greene's death, and therefore since the *True Tragedy* is in immediate sequence to *The First Part of the Contention,* that play must be still earlier. The inference is that both plays are early works of Shakespeare. To deny that Greene refers to Shakespeare is to be incapable of inference, to make nonsense of what Greene says, and to ignore his enmity to the players. If more is wanted to prove that the *Contention* and the *True Tragedy* are actually plays by Shakespeare, one has only to remember that they are the same plays as *2* and *3 Henry VI* and that quartos and folio run together line for line in all essential passages in the telling of the same stories. If Shakespeare wrote *2* and *3 Henry VI,* he also wrote the *Contention* and the *True Tragedy.*

There is also one bit of external evidence for a late revision by Shakespeare of the Henry VI plays. Tucker Brooke discovered[18] that Talbot's epitaph as given in Richard Crompton's *Mansion of Magnanimitie* (1599) is almost exactly repeated in the folio version of *1 Henry VI* (IV, vii, 65–71). Josephine Pearce's discovery of the same epitaph in Roger Cotton's *An Armor of Proofe* (1596) makes the borrowing more feasible by placing the publication of the epitaph somewhat earlier. The three parts of *Henry VI* are in some respects uniform in style, since they agree in their sequential or cyclic features.

1 Henry VI in particular shows what may be evidences of adaptation to the events of *2* and *3 Henry VI*, and some light may come from discrimination of sources. C. F. Denny[19] met with some success in showing that the parts of *1 Henry VI* that go back to an older tradition, and that hence were presumably composed earlier, were derived from the chronicles of Hall or Grafton, and the parts that connect the play with later plays in the sequence were derived from Holinshed. Lucille King[20] carried the discrimination of chronicle sources of all of the Henry VI plays somewhat further with results at least not incompatible with the idea that the parts thought to be revisional tend to appear in Holinshed.

The important work, however, is that of C. T. Prouty,[21] who by comparing the texts of the *Contention* and *2 Henry VI* arrives at a well-based conclusion that the folio play is Shakespeare's revision of the quarto. He does not believe that the *Contention* was written by Shakespeare, and in this opinion is probably wrong, but one cannot see how his case for the revision of the folio text, and by Shakespeare, can be disputed. On the grounds of structure, further and deeper characterization, staging, and style, Prouty argues that the blank verse, particularly in long speeches, is excellent and of the quality to be expected in the later histories and comedies. He finds no so-called evidence of memorial reconstruction and dismisses it. In general, the relation of the texts of the *Contention* and *2 Henry VI* may be left in Prouty's hands. There are other variants besides those due to revision, but they seem chargeable to actors and printers. Prouty's work also affords an easy solution to the problem of the texts of the *True Tragedy* and *3 Henry VI*. There is little or no evidence of cutting in either quarto, the stories told being equally complete in quartos and folio, so complete in fact that the earlier plays may always have been short.

The general theory is that Shakespeare's great success with *Richard III, Richard II, 1* and *2 Henry IV,* and *Henry V* caused a revival of interest in the reign of Henry VI and induced him to revise the *Contention* and the *True Tragedy* in a thoughtful and effective way, so that they would occupy a proper place in the grand subject of the civil wars of the fifteenth century. It will be noticed that the *Contention* and the *True Tragedy* are not named for kings, but, like *A Mirror for Magistrates*, present special subjects and characters. With *Richard III, King John*, and *Henry IV* there came plays named for kings, and the amplification and perfection of these early plays into a great trilogy dealing with the Wars of the Roses was properly named for Henry VI.[22] It is a mere speculation, but there is a fitness in the idea that an early Talbot play, such as that mentioned by Nashe in *Pierce Penilesse his Supplication to the Diuell* (1592), whether by Shakespeare or not, served as the basis of the greatly revised *1 Henry VI*.

As to detail of differences and agreements between the *True Tragedy* and *3 Henry VI* it is not possible here to give more than a few selected cases:

I, i.—The texts agree very closely. In some cases Q preserves original readings, although it has some single-line omissions that may be due to faulty printing. On the other hand, F has three poetical expansions. One of them (ll. 216–31) is clearly marked as an addition; perhaps also another that appears in ll. 241–48. The text of Q, except for one of the single-line omissions, reads perfectly, and it has several passages special to itself.

I, ii.—The part of Richard in F is certainly emphasized in this scene; the lines given him (ll. 16–34) are in the rhetorical style that often appears in passages special to F.

II, i.—This scene is devoted to the news of York's death and the gathering of the Yorkists. The episode of the three suns, ll. 1–42, appears somewhat differently in the two texts, F being the fuller and smoother, although Q is entirely adequate. In F Edward makes an opening speech, and Richard's reply is amplified in F with five lines of rhetorical verse and two lines (ll. 23–24) of characteristic vulgarity. The Messenger gives a different account (ll. 42 ff.) in F of York's capture and death. Richard's comment in F (ll. 79–86) characteristically substitutes ferocity for grief. After the entrance of Warwick and Montague (l. 94) the two texts are almost identical except for the omission, probably by the Q printer, of two single lines in Q and with also the intrusion into that text, as often, of occasional epithets such as appear in acting versions. The dialogue between the Yorkists (ll. 201–9) differs slightly in the two texts. There is some casual revision in F, for which a new conception of Richard's character seems the only plausible explanation. However, some of Richard's speeches that appear in both texts seem loyal and normal, as, for example, ll. 96–188, where his admiration of Warwick is genuine.

III, ii (Edward IV and Lady Grey).—The scene runs parallel in the two texts with, however, some additions in F. It is significant that the vulgar and cynical attitude of Richard is a main feature of the parts peculiar to F, this being properly accompanied by evidences of the sensuality of Edward IV. In this scene the principal motive for revision comes into the open, namely, the reflection in *3 Henry VI* of the Richard made familiar to us in *Richard III*. The cue for this, to be sure, is present in Q, which makes clear Richard's ambition to gain the crown for himself, but in F we have super-emphasis. In a long soliloquy in F (ll. 123–95) we have the actual Machiavel. How all traces of this startling idea could have been obliterated by process of cutting or reporting I fail to understand. This most significant feature must be part of a revision. Richard's sense of inferiority because of his deformity and of his unpopularity is present in Q, where he announces his desire for the crown and enumerates the persons who stand between him and it; but there is lacking in Q that complete and conscious evil that appears in the Richard of *Richard III*. He compares himself in Q not to Machiavelli, but to Cataline! In the light of this and other passages in F and not in Q devoted to the development of Richard's evil character, can anyone doubt that *3 Henry VI* was revised by Shakespeare after the full conception of *Richard III* had been formed in his mind?

IV, vi (Henry and Richmond).—In Q the scene appears after Edward's invasion. Q may preserve the original order, since Henry's capture included in the scene would have occurred after Edward's victory. This is borne out by what looks like a full-length revision of the scene in F. It is very short in Q. In F it is united with the news of Edward's escape; in Q with the preparations for the battle of Barnet. F seems to show a full and painstaking revision foreshadowing the future greatness of Richmond as Henry VII. It celebrates the virtues of the young earl in words almost entirely new. King Henry lays his hand on Richmond's head and bestows on him a prophet's blessing, and Somerset provides for the boy's escape to Brittany. One can hardly doubt that this scene, which looks ahead to *Richard III*, was developed in F because of its support of the Tudor succession, a purpose everywhere present in England from Polydore Vergil on. In F it is given a new and happier setting than in Q, and is part of the emphasis on the sweetness and holiness of King Henry VI that appears throughout the last scenes of *3 Henry VI*.

V, iv (Margaret at Tewkesbury).—The Queen's great speech (ll. 1–49, 73–82), much shorter in Q, seems revisional and may be intended to emphasize her brave and warlike spirit. Q deals with immediate detail. In Q, moreover, Prince Edward's speeches are much longer than in F. The texts, although differing greatly, are both sound.

V, v (the murder of Prince Edward).—The versions run parallel. Clarence and Richard stab the prince (ll. 39–40) in F, following Holinshed, and there are other slight signs of revision.

There are other plays by Shakespeare with quarto and folio versions that might be worth considering from the point of view of this chapter; but those described here—*Romeo and Juliet, The Merry Wives of Windsor, Hamlet,* and the Henry VI plays— will serve to make the issue clear. This issue, which is of course open and in need of further study and thought, arises from the belief that wear on the stage affected all acted plays, and if one may judge from prompt-books, both printed and written, was a powerful, constantly operative agent of change and corruption. There are other plays in the Shakespeare canon, such as *Macbeth*, and many plays not by Shakespeare, such as *The Famous Victories of Henry V*, that in all probability have suffered degeneration on the stage, but there exist no versions with which the texts can be

compared. We therefore content ourselves with those here presented. We do not of course deny that faulty printing contributed
to the faults of "bad" quartos; but we believe that poor printing
alone is insufficient to account for what we find and that stage
corruption, being more varied and violent, must have entered into
the process of alteration and degeneration.

Stage degeneration thus constitutes a continuum from mere
ordinary and unimportant changes in dramatic texts to those that
work serious injury. To seize upon a few of the worst cases, make
of them a distinct class, and account for them speculatively as due
to piracy, stenography, or reporting is to truncate the continuum
and violate the principles of inductive reasoning.

CHAPTER 3

INADEQUATE METHODOLOGY IN
TEXTUAL CRITICISM

THERE is at this time a concept and practice of classical textual criticism that, brought over too absolutely into the field of Shakespearean and other Elizabethan texts, is causing both error and confusion. Its adoption is in line with the now questioned positivism of half a century or more ago, a time when scientific knowledge and theory were thought of as unshakable fact out of which, as from building stones, a perfect structure of knowledge and truth was in process of building. Relativistic philosophy has modified this positivistic ideal, so that so-called scientific principles are now regarded merely as working bases for the further discovery of truth. In the field of Shakespearean criticism the situation is a little worse than the blind acceptance of accredited scientific truth, since textual critics have sometimes failed to do justice to the breadth and efficacy of the textual criticism they have adopted.

Emendation or the attempt to correct and improve texts is an old practice. It has usually been an effort to restore what an author wrote. Emendation has had in it, from the beginning until its latest formulation into a system, an element of choice in which the emendator put himself for the nonce into the place of the author. This effort, in spite of a heterogeneity that has overloaded the Shakespeare Variorum with nonsense, is actually a better method of finding the truth than any erroneous or misunderstood scientific theory; for it at least gives a scholar of knowledge and intelligence a chance to exercise his enlightened judgment.

For ages the texts of ancient secular and religious works passed down from one copyist to another, although now and then enterprising scholars made efforts to produce editorially better texts. The turning point came with Karl Lachmann, who, in his edition of the New Testament in 1842, discovered the significance of common errors and laid down other principles of the criticism of ancient texts. He and his followers thus founded a new science with which there is little fault to be found. But note that the formal textual criticism of the classics operates by means of groups or families of versions back toward an archetype or supposedly perfect original from the hand of an author, and is based on the sequential copying of one manuscript or printed version from another.[1]

Such a system, correct as it is, does not and cannot apply without adaptation to all dramatic texts. Mystery plays when carried back to their origins disappear in tropes or tiny Latin *ordines*; the plays that we have before us are an aggregate of the work of many hands at many times, or, at best, some extensive redaction by a usually unknown reviser. Mystery plays were in process of composition for hundreds of years. We may sometimes be able to tear the compositions apart and with reasonable assurance determine stages of amplification; but in trying to describe textual relations and understand the interrelation of versions, we are forced to introduce other considerations than mere variants due to sequential transcription. The significance of common errors, a matter too often neglected in the criticism of Shakespearean texts, still holds, as do other appropriate principles of the criticism of classical texts.

There is nothing rigid or unintelligent in these principles as developed by classical scholars. The system makes ample allowance for every sort of special feature that may have appeared in the experience of a transmitted text, such as problems of collation, accidental resemblances among texts, intermixture or conflation, influence of nonexistent versions, and the nature of *testimonia*. It provides for every sort of subsidiary aid that it needs—translation into other languages, casual quotation, imitation, and ancient commentary. It studies causes of corruption, not only erroneous emendation, but errors of eye, mind, and hands; also misreadings, haplography, dittography, phonetic confusion, metrical dislocation, and wrong words. Classical textual criticism is adapted to its purposes and serves them well. Trouble comes when this system is applied mechanically to modern dramatic texts without allowance for the experiences through which they have passed and is so poorly understood that it becomes merely a matter of the priority of variants. The fact is that the texts of Elizabethan plays were not transmitted from copyist to copyist throughout the centuries, but came into existence in other ways.

In view of the scholarly breadth of the system of classical textual criticism, the same obligation rests on us to examine the special conditions that existed in Elizabethan times and the customs and influences that were then at work. If these forces had affected classical texts, allowance would have been made for them. Let us consider, for example, the customary ways of supplying manuscripts to dramatic companies, ways that seem normally to have brought into existence two versions of a new play: the author's original manuscript and a clean copy of it. The author's original may reasonably be supposed often to have been in a more or less disordered state. The problem would be simpler if the author's original had been destroyed or thrown away, but such copies seem sometimes to have survived and to have found their way into the hands of publishers. If the author's original manuscript was itself the revision of an older form of the play, the problem is further complicated.[2] Moreover, in the making of a clean copy for submission to the censor and for the use of the company, changes might be introduced, especially, one would think, if the author made the clean copy himself.

The clean copy became the authorized playbook of the company, and, when it got into the hands of the prompter and the actors, more changes were in store for it. These are not speculations; the evidence is written in prompt-books for everyone to see. Plays became subject to what may be called stage degeneration, a force that operated continually to a degree proportioned to the amount of use on the stage and to the competency of the actors who played the plays. Even so, the early and normal vicissitudes of plays are not over. Certain plays might be cut down for acting, and shortened versions may, for all we know, have been acted in London theaters; in any case they were used by traveling companies in the provinces, where acting was on a lower level than in the city because of the ignorance, poverty, and lack of skill of the players and the limited numbers in the troupes. Such plays got into print, and the textual results are sometimes bad; and yet these bad texts are often respectable in origin and not infrequently tell us what the dramatist actually wrote.

All of these special circumstances, and no doubt others, need to be taken into consideration in the textual history of Elizabethan plays, and formal textual criticism is inadequate unless this is done. We have to reckon with multiple versions and how they came into existence, with revisions, and the disregard of an author's words if the copyist, the printer, or, especially, the actor or the prompter decided to change them, add to them, or omit them. This is only a way of saying that nothing short of the completest possible knowledge will serve our turn—no mechanical systems, no hasty classifications, no mere theorizing, however authoritative.

Of course if the same readings, whether by unmistakable identity or community in error, appear in two different texts of the same work and one text is known to be earlier than the other, it would seem to follow logically that the later text is derived from the earlier. This is a normal inference. But a mechanical application of the principle of priority, one that fails to take into account all appertaining circumstances, may result in error, since in these special circumstances textual agreement may have come about by other means than transcription; that is, the text of earlier date may have had no influence whatever on the text of later date.

This is important in the textual criticism of Shakespeare, nineteen of whose plays come down to us as single publications in quarto, and eighteen of these appear also in the First Folio of 1623. This gives rise to problems of discrimination, since it sometimes happens that what are apparently original readings in quartos are merely corrections in reprints. These quarto readings are earlier in date than the folio, and since they precede the folio in time, it has been natural enough for scholars to conclude that the later versions were derived from the earlier ones. What should be pointed out is that there were certain conditions affecting the earlier quarto texts that may, and in some cases actually do, show that the priority of these quarto texts is an unrelated priority. This would affect the inference that certain of the folio texts were printed from quartos. The matter is important, and if the inference is wrong, which in some cases it certainly is, the texts of whole plays are vitiated. The facts relating to some of the plays that have been thus misunderstood are extremely plain; but with others to which the theory has been hastily applied the circumstances are doubtful and need re-examination.[3]

Shakespearean texts, as said above, come down to us as quarto and folio publications and not as versions resulting from transcription. In point of fact, folio versions seem prevailingly to have been printed from playhouse manuscripts, and at least some quarto versions seem to be based on the author's originals or on revisions of those originals. These facts complicate the problem, but at the same time throw light on it. To understand the issues we must realize, first, that both quarto versions when they were reprinted and folio versions when they were in the hands of the players or the printers were liable to alteration by other people besides the author or the copyist. Playhouse manuscripts or prompt copies, the texts of many of which were subsequently published in the First Folio, were subject to change when they were put on the stage and whenever they were revived. There is no mystery about this; these alterations have long been recognized and frequently described. The prompter marked the text for his own use; it underwent changes for casting; sometimes it was shortened; and sometimes the actual language was made simpler and more colloquial. Such changes are considerable, but are usually easy to recognize.[4]

Second, the reprinting of quartos was not a process of mere reproduction, since printers allowed themselves or were allowed considerable freedom in making changes. Their purpose was no doubt improvement; but they not only made new errors but a surprising number of wrong corrections, and also, by common-sense methods, restorations of original readings. Such textual restorations in reprinted quartos were obviously earlier than 1623, and when agreements in text between quartos and the folio were observed, they were often seized upon, by a too narrowly interpreted textual criticism of the classics, as evidence that the folio text had been set up from some earlier quarto and not from a playhouse manuscript; whereas there may have been no contacts whatever between such reprints and the copy for the folio. The relatively small number of textual agreements on which the theory that folio texts were printed from quarto texts rests may thus have come about from the casual corrections of the printers of reprints. An important fact is that the folio texts supposed to be reprinted from quartos never repeat the often numerous errors and false emendations special to the texts from which they are supposed to have been printed. In other words, there seems to be a violation of Lachmann's fundamental principle that community in error and not agreement in text is the determining factor. The reference is to emendation and not to actual or approximate identity. What I have in mind can be made clearer by a few examples.

Typical Cases

It has been believed by many scholars since the appearance of the Cambridge edition (1865) that the folio version of *Romeo and Juliet* was printed from the third quarto of 1609. In the text he was resetting from Q2, the printer of Q3 made a few common-sense corrections that restored Shakespeare's original text. This was in 1609; the folio text was printed probably in 1622; 1609 is earlier than 1622; therefore F must have got those readings from Q3 by using it as copy. The Cambridge editors give very little evidence for their opinion and ignore the fact that if Q3 had been used as copy for F, many special markings and errors that appear in Q3 would have appeared in F.

There are six of these simple corrections: I, ii, 104: Q2 *shewes*, Q3F *seemes*; III, iv, ll: Q2 *shees meeued*, Q3F *she is meeued*: III, v, 182: Q2 *liand*, Q3F *allied*; III, v 128: Q2 *Prates*, Q3F *pratest*; V, iii, 163: Q2 *drunk . . . left*, Q3F *drink*

. . . *left*; and V, iii, 209: Q2 *now earling down*, Q3F *now early down*. Besides these, there are four or five corrections of mere blunders that have no significance, but there is one possible common error: IV, iv, 10: Q2 *lesser*, Q3F *lesse*. There is no difference in meaning, and the matter is doubtful. Q3 was printed from a revision of an earlier form of the play and therefore retains many stage directions, but the difference between them and those of F are not accounted for. The directions are fuller and more practical in F, and one does not see how they could have come from anything except a playbook.

A faulty theory demands many defenses, and great ingenuity has been exercised in support of the one under consideration. The fact that many folio versions show evidence, especially in their stage directions, that they were printed from prompt-books has caused difficulty, since quarto versions are not marked in this way, or are differently marked. To meet this inconsistency it has been conjectured that the quarto supposed to have been used as folio copy had itself been used as a prompt-book and had been marked up to meet the needs of presentation and the preferences of actors.[5] A variant of this theory is to the effect that Heminge and Condell in preparing the copy for the First Folio caused a printed quarto to be collated with and corrected from an official playbook. To support this the anachronistic and rather feeble idea is put forward that printers greatly preferred setting type from printed copy to setting from copy written in the secretary hand. Scholars who have not had much experience in reading Elizabethan handwriting would naturally feel this way, but, after all, it was part of the printer's trade to learn to read secretary script, which was the means of written communication in the age.

The attempt to prove that the folio text of *Richard II* was set from a quarto is so full of contrivance as to be absurd. We shall use it as a further illustration of the uncertainty of the theory under consideration. The play was entered in the Stationers' Register to Andrew Wise on August 29, 1597, and quarto editions show a disposition to restore original readings, and when in a full were issued by him in 1597 and twice in 1598. These reprints court held on June 25, 1603, the ownership was transferred to Matthew Law, the reprints continue to improve—Q4 (1608) and Q5 (1615). The corrections of the text are again simple matters and there are new errors, but, in general, the intelligence of Wise's and Law's printers makes itself felt. A good many correct readings are restored that must have been in the Globe official copy and later appeared in the folio. If this natural assumption seems unwarranted, let us consider the matter in more detail.

The third quarto, identified by A. W. Pollard and edited by him in 1916,[6] brought up the question of the source of the folio text. He saw that Q1 had to be counted in on any operation of printing from a quarto, as indeed he might, since with or without the support of other quartos Q1 retains 90 original readings not appearing in F. It is in sole disagreement with F in 16 cases. Q2 makes 54 mistaken attempts to improve Q1 that do not appear in F, but makes 23 correct changes that do. We must therefore include Q2 among the quartos necessary (according to theory) to establish the folio text. Q3 makes 23 erroneous changes, but has 9 agreements with F. These agreements were so impressive that Pollard fixed on Q3 as the quarto from which F was set up. We cannot leave out Q4, since it presents along with 20 wrong alterations at least 2 and maybe 3 valid changes, and Q5 has, along with 24 mistaken corrections, 5 and perhaps 6 agreements with F so significant to Hasker[7] that he made the extraordinary suggestion that two leaves from Q5 had been inserted in a copy of Q3 to provide a text to be collated with a theatrical manuscript so that it might serve for the printing of F.

This relation is simply too complicated for reality. It would require a full set of all quartos with persons to collate them—in other words, a large clerical staff with one or more editors specifically instructed to close their eyes to the many errors and mistaken attempts at correction in all the quartos. Such conditions are not on record in that age and that enterprise, when little importance was attached to textual niceties either in acting or in printing. The whole undertaking is made implausible by the simple fact that Heminge and Condell had at hand an official playbook of *Rich-*

ard II that, being sent to the printers, answers every problem that arises, since it was one of the "True Originall Copies" that the purveyors said they had supplied. The folio preserves 16 original readings as against Q1, agrees with Q1 alone in 24, and against all quartos has 50. It supplies 51 substantive errors of its own. How could these readings have got into the First Folio unless they came from a manuscript? No collation however freakish could have supplied them, and one looks in vain for any motive.

Finally, if the folio printer had any quarto in front of him, surely he could not have failed to give a better representation of the document he was printing. Why did he leave out 50 excellent lines in the quartos that are not in the folio? If the imaginary quarto was one in use as a prompt copy, these omitted lines would be part of the play, and let it be remembered that the integrity of the text of Q1 is attested by 36 unquestionably original readings. Extended and meticulous care in doing unnecessary and unnatural things is absurd; for there are no reasons why the text of the folio version of *Richard II* may not have been printed, according to custom, from the book of the play in the hands of the theatrical company.

Carrying back into the early seventeenth century the meticulous textual scholarship of the modern world is anachronistic. If any such operation could have been effected, it would have been costly as well as unnecessary. In some cases, moreover, there are actual substantial barriers in the way of the theory we have been considering.

For example, one wonders if scholars who write with such assurance about the printing of the folio version of *King Lear* from a corrected copy of Q1 know what that supposition involves. The alterations that would be called for in the Q1 text are overwhelming. In Q1 there are mislineations of verse, some prose printed as verse, and hundreds of lines of verse printed as prose; also a great many verbal variants, some in F due to actors and some in both texts due to different misreadings of handwriting. Punctuation is widely different. There are evidences of revision in F that do not appear in Q1, which has 300 lines, including one whole scene (IV, iii), that do not appear in F. There are actually 100 lines in F that do not appear in Q1. To prepare such a quarto as copy for the folio would require at least 2,000 alterations—some of them long and difficult—not counting the markings necessary to correct mislineations of verse and to alter prose into the form of verse. Could these things have been done in limited space on the soft paper of a printed quarto? And if they could, is it not preposterous to think that any printer with such a document before him could have produced so orderly a text as the folio? Add to the difficulty and labor of such an operation that it was entirely unnecessary, for of course the theater had an authorized playbook of *King Lear*, and of course they sent it, as they sent others, to Jaggard and Blount to be printed.

In this chapter we have so far considered three plays whose problems may be regarded as typical: simple cases in which compositor's corrections in reprinted quartos have misled textual critics, complicated cases that have made it necessary for critics to invent explanations in order to save the theory, and what may be described as physical impossibilities. In addition, half a dozen or more other important plays whose textual history is vital to their correct treatment by editors must be examined. The matter is important.

Lachmann's discovery of the significance in textual criticism of agreement in error is not a mere piece of information; it is the only means by which the descent of manuscripts or printed versions can be certainly determined. The reason for this is that classical and other manuscripts and printed versions transmitted from copyist to copyist or printer to printer were continually subject to emendation by scribes, printers, and scholars. Such correction was great in amount and often restored original readings by the application of ordinary, often trained, intelligence to the version undergoing reproduction. Lachmann saw that such casual restorations of original readings have no necessary value in determining the history and descent of the work in question and that only common errors have significance. It is obvious that corrections by printers of the reprints of Shakespearean quartos belong to this class of casual corrections of texts. Such agreements have no necessary significance, whereas agreements in error might have. Each case is no doubt special, but there is little or no evidence that, in determining the important question of whether a given text in the First Folio was printed from the playhouse manuscript or from a printed quarto, Shakespeare scholars have been aware of Lachmann's principle.

They have apparently found agreements between the folio text and some specific quarto reprint and decided without further investigation that the folio text was set up from that particular quarto. In simple cases, such as that of *Romeo and Juliet,* the decision is merely wrong, and when it proceeds from a competent authority, it merely causes confusion (of course if incompetently presented the harm is greater). In other cases where the folio text shows on its face that it was printed from the Globe promptbook, the confusion is still greater and the error more harmful. Such decisions frequently cause the invention of circumstances to account for matters that came about in the normal routine of the playhouse and the printshop. There are even cases where the folio text shows errors derived from the misreading of handwriting, so that further circumstances have to be invented to account for these errors. The utterly fictitious idea that printers demanded printed rather than handwritten copy was mentioned above. These reprinters of quartos actually made more false corrections than true corrections; and if these reprinted quartos were used as copy for the setting of the folio text, one asks in vain why these multifarious errors of the printer of the reprinted quartos do not appear in the folio text. Certainly some of them would have been reproduced by the folio printer, and if they had been, we should know what we are doing. The fact that erroneous corrections by quarto printers were not to some degree picked up and followed by the printers of the folio is on its face a refutation of the whole theory. It is unscholarly to introduce an imaginary body of twentieth-century experts into the early seventeenth century in order that they might settle matters that at that time would have had no great importance. Another fact that is ignored, in spite of its bearing on the question, is of particular importance in cases where there is only one quarto and it is insisted that that quarto was used as copy for the folio text. The fact is that, in the texts in question, the fair copy supplied to the theater was made from the same manuscript from which the quarto was printed. It was often in these instances Shakespeare's foul papers of a revision, and of course the two versions would be very much alike. The result of this misunderstanding is a shocking confusion in the determination of the texts of a considerable number of Shakespeare's greatest plays.

When scholars have happened to see textual agreements between reprinted quartos and the folio text, they have tended to conclude at once that the folio text, which is later in date than the corrected quarto text, was certainly set up from the quarto.[8] *Romeo and Juliet,* discussed above, presents such a case. When other quartos, reprinted quartos of the play in question, have come by the casual process of correction noted in *Romeo and Juliet* into agreement with the folio, it does not help the perplexity to have the scholar deftly suppose that some invented editor has consulted the later quarto and introduced the better reading into the favored text before it was used as folio copy; or to imagine in other cases that a single leaf or, if necessary, two leaves from a later quarto have been bound in with a copy of the favored quarto.

The result of this tinkering is, as said above, a shocking confusion in the determination of the true texts of a considerable number of Shakespeare's plays. A restatement of the facts with reference to this group of plays will make the issue clear: the quarto texts of *Hamlet* (Q2), *Romeo and Juliet* (Q2) and *Love's Labour's Lost,* as can be inferred from their title pages, were set up from Shakespeare's foul papers of a revision of earlier forms. There is evidence to indicate that the quartos of *Much Ado about Nothing* and *1* and *2 Henry IV* had undergone revision before they were printed, although there is no statement to that effect. With the addition of certain complicating factors *A Midsummer-Night's Dream* follows the same pattern. This same circumstance of revision of earlier versions may have a bearing on the problems of *The Merchant of Venice,* the three parts of *Henry VI,* and *Richard III.* This conjecture is not out of line with Elizabethan

customs and the supply of plays to publishers. It would follow
that such quarto and folio versions are much alike. A much more
definite attendant circumstance seems also to be overlooked;
namely, that fair copies of revised plays would have to be made
for submission to the censor and for the use of the dramatic company; also, and this is extremely important, that these fair copies,
bearing the license of the censor, became the official playbooks or
"originals" of the dramatic company.

Other Problems

Of the plays with which we are concerned *Romeo and Juliet*,
Richard II, and *King Lear* have been considered as regards the
contention that a quarto was used as folio copy. The case of
Romeo and Juliet seemed to be a simple blunder, that of *King
Lear* to demand an impossible operation, and that of *Richard II*
to be a figment of the imagination. All three of them seem to
call for quite unnecessary operations, and the case of *Richard II*
in anachronism and sheer complexity made absurd the idea
that the folio version could have been set from any quarto
whatsoever. We found that, taking the conjecture on the terms
of its advocates, a great staff of editors and scholars would have
been needed to make collations and expert choices, notwithstand-
ing the fact that such meticulous scholarship was simply nonexistent in publication circles in the early seventeenth century.
We proved that such a staff would have had to have at hand all
five quartos and would have had to be instructed not to involve
themselves with Lachmann's theory of contrary instances; that
is, they were to avoid all of the many, sometimes rather plausible,
false emendations made by quarto printers at the same time that
they were making some correct guesses. Such imaginary scholars
would moreover have had to be deeply read in Shakespeare as a
world classic, although he was not so regarded at that time. The
whole imagined theory seemed to have the usual two primary
objections: it was unnecessary, since simply sending the authorized copy to the folio printers would answer every need and question; and, secondly, such editorial action is characteristic of the
twentieth and not of the early seventeenth century.

A few more texts remain to be examined. We must consider some relatively simple cases and some others that are more complicated. Let us begin with *Love's Labour's Lost.*

A quarto edition of *Love's Labour's Lost* was published in 1598 as "newly corrected and augmented," and the play was included in the folio of 1623. This looks on its face as if *Love's Labour's Lost* had followed the same career as the second quartos of *Romeo and Juliet* and *Hamlet*; that is, Shakespeare revised an earlier form of the play,[9] and the manuscript of his revision, having been transcribed as a fair copy for submission to the censor and the use of the company, fell, by agreement or otherwise, into the hands of publishers, who issued the quarto. The fair copy became the authorized playbook of the Lord Chamberlain's, later the King's, company, and printing the folio from the playhouse copy as modified by theatrical use would answer all questions and solve all problems—and be less expensive. A correct understanding of the textual history of *Troilus and Cressida* and of *Othello* is itself a refutation of the doctrine of quartos as folio copy. In the case of *Troilus and Cressida* we tried to show that the quarto text had been misclassified, since it seems to have been based on a transcription of the manuscript of the folio before it was marked up by the prompter and otherwise changed by its experience on the stage; so that we have, to begin with, the spectacle of two texts of the play as Shakespeare wrote it, the quarto printed in a careless way but unmarked for stage use and the folio plainly printed from a prompt-book, which of course was the official playhouse copy belonging to the King's company. There is no reason to think that these texts are not what they appear to be, and since they explain their entries in the Stationers' Register and the forms of their publications, there seems no reason to vary from normal practice by the intrusion of mere speculation. We refused to believe that the folio version of *Othello*, the finest text in all Shakespeare, was botched up and printed from a quarto (1622) formerly acted on the stage and greatly shortened.

In Chapter 2 an attempt was made to prove that the first quarto of *Hamlet* is a stage version of the play before it was revised into the form of Q2. This discovery, which has textual importance of its own, solves the problem of Q2 and reveals the interrelation of Q2 and F, since from it an inference can be made that F was not set up from a copy of Q2. A great deal of ingenuity has been expended in an effort to prove the opposite, but these two texts as they stand are clearly different. F was certainly printed from a manuscript, and it underwent revision, as did *King Lear*, probably when the fair copy was being made from the revised manuscript represented by Q2. The two versions, although derived from the same document, are so different that F could not have been printed from Q2.

With reference to *Richard II* we tried to explain an extreme position, in which the play underwent changes when it was acted or revised, but was on hand to be sent to Jaggard and Blount and published in the First Folio of 1623.

This seems to be a plain story, and yet nearly all introductions to *Love's Labour's Lost* and nearly all scholarly accounts of the play contain this statement: "There is no doubt that F was set up from Q." Some editors go further and explain why they are so positive in their opinion. In the quarto (V, i, 57) for the word *venewe* (venue) we find *vene we*, and the same error in the same form appears in the folio. This, apparently, settles the matter. One account puts it thus: " Now it is inconceivable that the same accident should have happened in the same place of the same work in two independent printings." This may be granted, but the question is, did it happen in this way? There are at least two things that have not been observed by these editors and by the many commentators who say, "There is no doubt," etc. If one looks without theoretical sophistication at the facts, one sees that both versions, the quarto and the fair copy that in normal routine became the playbook of the company and the copy for the folio, are derived from exactly the same document, namely, Shakespeare's manuscript of his revision of an earlier form of *Love's Labour's Lost*. Therefore, if these routine happenings are accepted, the error in question appeared in Shakespeare's manuscript and was carried over first into the fair copy and, secondly, into the quarto. Wrong divisions of words are by no means rare in hand-written copy.

One may call this an accident or a temptation to error if one likes, but there are unnoticed external circumstances that may have caused this double blunder. The word is so divided as to cause the last two letters to stand as the common pronoun *we*. The speech in which the mistake occurs is by Don Armado, whose specialty is odd language. It is not beyond the range of possibility that both the transcriber of the fair copy and the printer of the quarto, seeing the word "we" associated with a combination of letters, accepted it as it stood and left the meaning to the Don.

But we do not rest the case on this. To settle a complicated problem of textual relations on a single instance is to violate an established principle of textual discrimination: texts should be viewed as wholes and not classified according to what may be accidental criteria. McKerrow makes this perfectly clear and convincing.[10] The folio text of *Love's Labour's Lost* is a respectable document that sets right most of the errors of the quarto printer.[11] It was based on Shakespeare's manuscript before the quarto was printed from it. The copyist did a better job than the printer. The folio text is adequately but not elaborately marked for stage use. For example, it attends carefully to entrances and exits and most other needs of performance.[12] We seem therefore to have a situation quite in line with normal practice with nothing to interfere with it except one misinterpreted crux. To insist that the folio was set up from the quarto is to involve ourselves in unnecessary complications, and we prefer a simple explanation and see no reason for anything else.

Much Ado about Nothing exists also in only two early texts, a quarto of 1600 and the folio of 1623. One would say that it presents a problem of quarto-folio relationship quite like those of *Hamlet* and *Romeo and Juliet*, except for the fact that the title page of the quarto does not say, as in the other cases, that it is a revision. It happens, however, that *Much Ado about Nothing* shows signs of having been revised; Dover Wilson makes it clear that the quarto was printed from Shakespeare's revision of an earlier form of the play.[13] We thus have the same sequence: Shakespeare's manuscript of his revision was copied for submission to the censor and the use of the players; it became the authorized playbook of the company; it underwent further changes during its experience on the stage; and it was sent to Jaggard and Blount to be published in the First Folio. Meantime, after this copy had been made, Shakespeare's manuscript, being no longer of use or importance to its owners, fell into the hands of Andrew Wise and William Aspley and was published in quarto form in 1600. If this customary routine is accepted, it will be seen that the fair copy and the printed quarto are both versions of the same emended manuscript and would normally be very much alike.

To this we should add the possibly suspicious circumstance that *Much Ado about Nothing* was one of the plays entered in the Stationers' Register, on May 27, 1600, to be stayed. This entry has been taken to mean, no doubt correctly, that the Lord Chamberlain's company tried to prevent the publication of this and the other plays mentioned; and it may be added that they were possibly aware that Wise and Aspley had Shakespeare's revised manuscript in their possession and were about to publish it. If so, their attempt to prevent the publication must either have failed or have led to an agreement.[14]

There is no support for the belief that the folio text was set from the quarto rather than from the playhouse prompt-book except the anachronistic argument that early seventeenth-century printers would have demanded printed instead of handwritten copy. Since the folio text bears the marks of use on the stage to a greater degree than does the text of the quarto, scholars who are determined to have the folio printed from the quarto have been obliged to introduce a well known probably invented cause; namely, that a quarto to be used as copy for the folio was collated with the playhouse manuscript in order that it might serve as folio copy. However, no one who stops to think would believe that the publishers of the folio would have cared a button whether the play they printed had prompter's stage directions or not. A romantic variant of this is to have the quarto used as a prompt-book in the theater. Some point has been made of the closeness of agreement between the two texts that have come down to us. One simply says "Why not?," since the two texts were originally versions of the same manuscript—one by the maker of the fair copy and the other by the printer of the quarto.

The early versions of *The Merchant of Venice* cause perplexity. James Roberts, who is believed to have been on friendly terms with the players, entered the play in the Stationers' Register on July 22, 1598. On October 28, 1600, it was transferred "by Consent of Master Robertes" to Thomas Hayes (or Haies). In that entry in the Stationers' Register it is identified as an actual playbook by the phrase "A booke called the booke of" *The Merchant of Venice*. It was published by Hayes in 1600. In 1619 *The Merchant of Venice* was included in the attempted collection of Shakespearean plays (printed by William Jaggard), and this shows it in Jaggard's hands. Finally it appeared in the First Folio.

It is said without convincing justification that the folio text was set up from the first quarto, but our chief need is to know the reason for the publication of the first quarto, what it actually was and why it was available for publication. It was entered as a playbook and it is marked as such in the quarto, but the King's company must have had another playbook of their own, since *The Merchant of Venice* appears twice in the "Shaxberd" entries in the Revels Accounts.[15] The only thing we know of that would make a playbook dispensable, so that such a book might have been put into the hands of James Roberts, is a revision as in the three cases above. There is thus a possibility that the quarto was printed from a revised manuscript of which a fair copy had been made. And there have indeed been casual speculations that certain passages (mainly in prose) of *The Merchant of Venice* may be revisional, but the speculation is hazardous and has in its favor only the fact that it offers an explanation within normal custom of the nature and origin of the first quarto.

If the dramatic company had a licensed copy of *The Merchant of Venice*, as they certainly must have had, it would have been sent to the publishers of the First Folio. The argument that this was done is now familiar. The text of this playhouse copy, being itself a copy of the manuscript from which the first quarto was printed, would have closely resembled the text of the quarto. Indeed, it may have been better. It has full prompter's markings, which must have come from the stage. There was no reason why the official playbook should not have been sent to the folio printers, so that the whole question at issue here and above is whether these plays in the folio were set from doctored up quartos or from playhouse manuscripts. Most of them show evidence of the misreading of handwriting, and the argument that the whole business was troublesome, unnecessary, and expensive, although it may not meet with recognition, does not lose its force.

There seems little reason to call in question Dover Wilson's opinion that the first quarto of *A Midsummer-Night's Dream* had been revised by Shakespeare from an earlier form of the play.[16] If so, we may proceed for a certain distance with some confidence. The revised manuscript would, first of all, have been copied for the reasons so often stated, and this fair copy, after undergoing some alterations in the theater, would have been sent to the publishers for inclusion in the First Folio, but for a possible interference to be mentioned shortly. The foul papers of the revision, having lost their immediate usefulness to the players, would have been liable to fall into the hands of publishers for issue in quarto form, and this must have happened, since we have the quarto. *A Midsummer-Night's Dream* was entered in the Stationer's Register on October 8, 1600, and published by Thomas Fisher that same year.

As a printed version of the same manuscript from which the fair copy had been made, Q1 would resemble the theatrical version very closely, and this may be said of both the quarto and the folio as they stand. It does not seem necessary therefore, in view of this identity of origin, to imagine that the folio has been set from the quarto. Printing of the folio from the playhouse copy is a simpler and actually more satisfactory way in which to account for resemblances between these two texts. This would offer a clear solution to all problems but for the fact that, before the issue of the folio, Q1 had been reprinted in 1619 by William Jaggard in the attempted collection of Shakespeare's plays. Jaggard had thus a copy at hand, and some scholars have found in this fact evidence that Jaggard and Blount simply reset the text of this second quarto in the First Folio. This theory, however, is not adequate to account for what we find in F, which, although it has some features that may be derived from Q2, actually resembles Q1 more closely than it does Q2. There are of course passages in which F differs from both Q1 and Q2; in some of these cases F seems to have been set from manuscript, but, for the most part, the difference lies in the fact that F has abundant stage directions that do not appear in either quarto. Scholars have therefore resorted to the expedient of an imaginary copy of Q1 or Q2 that has been collated with a theatrical copy, presumably from the licensed copy belonging to the King's company. We are by now used to this argument, and we do not find it either necessary or probable. In this perplexity one has to content oneself with a moderate position: the official playbook was in the hands of Jaggard and Blount and served them as copy for the body of the play, although there are in F certain minor resemblances to Q2. In considering the problem one must remember that in all three early copies of *A Midsummer-Night's Dream* we have to do originally with one and the same version of the play.

An interesting and rather complicated situation is presented by the early texts of *Richard III*. Perhaps for lack of definite information the problem is not well understood.[17] *Richard III* seems to have been a popular play with bookbuyers, and there is an array of early texts. It was entered in the Stationers' Register to Andrew Wise on October 20, 1597. Then follow Q1 in 1597, printed by Valentine Sims for Andrew Wise; Q2, printed in 1598 by Thomas Creed for Andrew Wise; Q3 in 1598 with the same printer and publisher and represented unintelligibly as "Newly augmented." On June 25, 1603, *Richard III*, together with *Richard II* and *1 Henry IV*, was transferred from Andrew Wise to Matthew Law, and accordingly in 1605, Q4 was issued as printed by Thomas Creed for Matthew Law; in 1612, Q5 appeared with the same publisher and printer; and in 1622, Q6 as printed by Thomas Purfoot for Matthew Law. In 1623 *Richard III* was published in the First Folio in a text widely differing from the quartos. The reason for detailing the quarto publications is that the quartos of *Richard III*, along with those of *Richard II* and *1 Henry IV* (all in the hands of Wise and then Law), show a remarkable tendency to emend by common-sense methods the texts published and thus to restore original readings. They also make a good many mistaken emendations.

The manufacture of theories by which to account for differences among the quartos themselves and for the relation between the folio text and that of the quartos began with P. A. Daniel in 1883.[18] Since then there has been a drift among scholars toward the vague theory of memorial reconstruction with, however, considerable minor variations. The general belief of Patrick, Chambers, Greg, Miss Walker, and possibly Dover Wilson, is that the first quarto of *Richard III* is the product of reporting and is therefore in a sort of technical sense a "bad" quarto. One would hesitate to enter upon a subject so sparsely supported by fact, so theoretical, and yet so strongly supported by authority, but for two circumstances. First, Q1 presents, as Sir Walter Greg saw,[19] an excellent text so complete, so vigorous, and so independent that it is difficult to see how it could have been written down from memory by any group of actors. Second, it could hardly have been derived from the folio, since F, although covering the same ground, is different and continually so. F is more literary than Q1, more graceful, careful, and leisurely. It is as truly Shakespearean in its refinement as is Q1 in its bluntness. This may throw some light, however dim, on the problem, for there is more than one way to account for the differences between these two texts. Miss Walker, who is by no means indifferent to the significance of common error, uses that principle to degrade Q1, since if one wishes to establish the theory that Q1 is derived from F, every variant in Q1 becomes an error. Many scholars of note are firmly convinced that Q1 is so derived, and I am reluctant to go against their judgment; I wish only to point out that if in about 1597 Shakespeare had rewritten his great play in a finer literary style, a stage version of *Richard III* (and the quarto is a stage version) would have become superfluous and might therefore have come into Wise's hands to be entered and published by him. An even more plausible theory, which also demands separate acts of composition by Shakespeare himself for the folio and the quarto, is that when Shakespeare's company went into the country in the summer and autumn of 1596, Shakespeare wrote for them hastily but firmly a text to be acted on that tour. When they returned to London such a stage version, being no longer needed, might have been published as the first quarto. One feels apologetic about these conjectures; they are both, however, within the range of customary procedure, and in the field of the textual history of *Richard III* two more conjectures will perhaps do no harm.

Another theory with very strong support goes back to Alexander Schmidt,[20] who contended that the first 164 lines of III, i, and the end of the folio text from v, iii, 47 on, were set up from a copy of Q3. Schmidt's article calls for collations, and the areas selected for reproduction from Q3 seem to be those where there are the largest numbers of agreements in correct readings between F and Q3. There are other agreements with Q3 in F besides these; and when one observes that some scholars believe that F was printed mainly from a copy of Q6, or a combination of Q3 and Q6, one grows suspicious and thinks of those remarkable printers who worked for Matthew Law and in process of reprinting made so many remarkable restorations of text, not only in *Richard III*, but in *Richard II* and *1 Henry IV*. Schmidt's hypothesis, accepted by many scholars, calls for a damaged theatrical manuscript of the folio, but may, after all, have come about from the happy successes of these printers of reprints in the emendation of the texts on which they were at work.

Variants between all quartos and the folio of *Richard III* are legion, and one must demur, as in the case of *King Lear*, at the idea that any quarto text would be legible if it had had made on it the hundreds and hundreds of alterations that would be needed before it could serve as copy for the folio printers.[21]

In Chapter 1 it was suggested that there is something more
to be said from a strictly textual point of view about *1* and *2 Henry
IV* and their relation to the Dering version of *Henry IV*. It was
further suggested that it is incredible that any scholar who has
had to do with *1 Henry IV* and, especially, *2 Henry IV* and who
has read the Dering play could fail to see evidence that the Dering
play is a single drama antedating the two-part play and repre-
senting as it stands Shakespeare's original treatment of the wild
life of Prince Hal, his reformation, his winning of glory, and
his rejection of Falstaff, this being supported by certain scenes appearing in simple versions in the Dering play and in elaborately
revised forms in *2 Henry IV*. Of course these things could not be
if the Dering version were based, as it was thought to be, on the
fifth quarto of *1 Henry IV* published in 1613. There is no objection to a conviction that arises from an intelligent total view.
But the lines cited in Chapter 1 from the Dering version are certainly not selected and abridged from the standard version; they
are different and obviously in an older and less highly developed
form. And the argument that abridgment does not proceed this
way, that it would on quite general grounds be impossible, besides
being stupid and unnecessary, to make any such condensation as
the Dering version out of the two-part play, is not to be cast aside.
But the matter can be carried further in order to show that there
are no textual obstructions to the acceptance of the new concept
of the Dering play. This will, at the same time, show the origin
of Halliwell's mistake. There is also the subsidiary question of
whether the folio versions of *1* and *2 Henry IV* were set from
quartos. It will mark the end of that tiresome but necessary
subject.

The textual problem involving the mistake in dating is simple
enough. The originator of the idea that the Dering version was
derived from the fifth quarto and was therefore to be dated after
1613 merely saw some agreements between Q5 and D and came
to his conclusion and has been obediently followed ever since. In
reprinting the fifth quarto of *1 Henry IV*, Law's clever printer
simply outdid himself as a shrewd corrector of texts. There are
many such agreements and Halliwell is not to be blamed. There

is no conjecture here, since Law's printers can be traced in their emendations all the way through from the second quarto in 1599 to the sixth in 1622.

It was made perfectly clear by Arthur Eustace Morgan[22] that *1* and *2 Henry IV* are revised plays; by drawing the Dering version into the discussion, we are attempting to show what the fundamental revision was. In view of what has been said in Chapter 1, it will perhaps serve our turn to give the results of a collation of the Dering text with *1 Henry IV*, in order to show how the mistake in dating the Dering manuscript after 1613, the date of the fifth quarto of *1 Henry IV*, came about. No evidence was found that any of the many wrong corrections that appear in reprinted quartos were taken over into the Dering text, although, as already pointed out, it is a practical impossibility that any copy, written or printed, could be made from any quarto without repeating at least some of these erroneous emendations.[23]

Q2 (1599) has eleven corrections or restorations of the original text, the comparison being with Q1. Q3 (1604) also has eleven. Q4 (1608) has six, Q5 (1613), seven, and Q6 (1622), one. Even Q8 (1639) has two, which probably came out of the printer's head. D is in agreement with these corrections. There are nine cases in which D seems to have original readings, either alone or in agreement with F only. Five of them seem to be unique. In four cases D agrees with F against all the quartos. One of these may be an agreement in error. There seem to be five outright errors in D, although two of them may be due to the misreading of handwriting. When D agrees with restorations of the original texts in these reprinted quartos, which it almost always does, it is usually in company with F. The inference here is not that D copied the correction as Halliwell thought it did, but that it had the correct reading already, it being actually older than the quarto in question. There is only one common error between Q5-8 and D, the error not appearing in F. It is in II, iii, 276: Q1-F *tired*, Q5-8 *tried*, D *tryed*. In l. 598 of the same act and scene we have Q1-3 *march*, Q4-8FD *match*, which may be an old error, since it appears in F, the word *match* being suggested by the phraseology of the line. II, iv, 228, Qq.D *roare* for Q1F *roard* is merely the common misreading of *e* for *d*, and Q4-8D *attend* (IV, iii, 70) is a variant form of Q1-3F *attended*. This is not a bad showing.

There are several passages in the Dering play that reveal actual differences from the text of *1 Henry IV* and not mere variants. It is hard to see how they could have come from the fifth quarto. For example:

I, i, 5-6:

Q: No more the thirsty entrance of this soile
            Shal dawbe her lips with her own childrens bloud.

D: No more the thirsty bosome of this land
            Shall wash herselfe with her own childrens bloud.

I, i, 25-27:

Q: Ouer whose acres walkt those blessed feet . . .
            For our advantage on the bitter crosse.

D: And force proude Mahomett from Palestine.

Or take the description of the robbery corresponding to II, ii, 80-100:

Prin. Ned: where ar our disguises
Poyn. Here, put on, put on:
Prin. So: Poynes looke vp the hill: see what is done there: At sea the greater fishe devoures the lesse: And on the land woulues liue by killing lambes: Now when the theeues haue bound the true men: and the true men rob'd the theeues agayne: it wilbe argument for a weeke: laughter for a time, and a good jest for ever. (Poynes returnes)
Poy. Come Hall goe: the theeues are diuiding the true mens goods.
Prin. Come suddenly, suddenly.

> *They two go out & rob* FALSTALFF *& the rest:*
> FALSTALFF & BARDOLF *runne away ouer the stage*
> *as* FALST. *goes he speakes,*
> O cowardly prince & Poynes, where ar they?

There are some marked differences, too, between the characters in the Dering version and those in the quartos and the folio.

Sir Walter Blunt takes Westmoreland's place in scene i and Prince John of Lancaster does further on. Gadshill is absent. Peto plays but a small part in D, and Poins often takes his place. Vernon does not appear in D, nor does the Archbishop of York.

We have, as usual, the contention that the folio version of *1 Henry IV* was set up from a quarto. The fifth quarto (1613) is the one favored, apparently on the ground that by that time Matthew Law's excellent printers had accumulated by common-sense methods a very considerable number of emendations that restored the original text. To this conclusion we make the same three objections. (1) The first quarto was probably set from Shakespeare's foul papers of his revision. The folio would have been set from a fair copy of that document, which became the authorized playbook of the Lord Chamberlain's, later the King's, company. This theatrical version, being used on the stage, would suffer some alterations; but as a copy of the same document that the quarto was printed from, the folio, except for the marks of its stage career, resembles the quarto very closely. It would have been customary, natural, and inexpensive to send this theatrical manuscript to the printers of the folio as one of the true original copies that Heminge and Condell say they sent. The supposition that it was so sent solves all difficulties.

(2) The questionable theory that the folio was set up from the fifth quarto arose from the fact that the printers for Matthew Law had made a number of skillful corrections in the text of the fifth quarto. Such a conclusion, however, can have no certainty, since it proceeds solely on the basis of agreements and is a violation of Lachmann's principle; and indeed the flaw in the argument is revealed by the nature of the textual corrections that Matthew Law's printers made. In this case they made false emendations as well as true ones. If the folio had been set from the fifth quarto, it would reflect these false corrections, and it does not.

(3) The folio has more and better stage directions than does the quarto. If it was set up from a quarto, where did it get these stage markings? This question does not stump these scholars,

since they set their fancies to work. Sometimes the folio comes out as a copy of a quarto used on the stage or, in its higher flights, it provides one or more textual experts who transfer to the fortunate quarto every mark on the face of a manuscript playbook, a matter that cannot have been of interest or importance to those in charge of the publication of Shakespeare's plays. The First Folio shows no policy with regard to alterations for staging, and has every sort of variety.

We are able to close rather hopefully this study of the hypothesis that in all cases where there exist two closely related texts, one in quarto and the other in folio form, the First Folio was always set up from a more or less specially altered copy of the quarto. In the case of *2 Henry IV*, the quarto was, in some current opinions, set from Shakespeare's foul papers, although it is not said that they were the foul papers of a revision, which of course they must have been. It is also affirmed by some authorities that the folio was set from a manuscript, as indeed it was, since a fair copy of foul papers had to be made for submission to the censor and the use of the players; that is, the folio was set from the playhouse manuscript or "original." Some great enthusiasts, however, hold out for collation and a skillful editorial preparation of a quarto to be used as folio copy.[24] Still, with one exception, the current trend of opinion about the texts of *2 Henry IV* is fairly simple and sound. Dover Wilson's treatment of the question seems reasonable. The scholarly idea is this: in the face of perplexities we should use what information we have and what we can find out. Occam's principle still holds good: when we are trying to solve problems, we should not invent or multiply causes (*entia*)—transcriptions, defective and patched manuscripts, conjectural situations, and preferences. In the textual criticism of *2 Henry IV* Occam's principle is shattered by the intrusion of a hypothetical transcript of the theatrical manuscript before it was printed. This argument should not be used unless it can be proved that no other explanation is possible. To say that the folio text of *2 Henry IV* is so superior in refinement to the quarto text that it must have been specially revised and purified needs to be checked by two things: first, the refinements of language and matter must be significantly discernible, since many, perhaps all, fair copies would show improvements over the foul papers from which they were made, especially, one would think, if made by the author or under his supervision. Second, there is a well known special reason why Shakespeare in this particular case should wish to put his best foot forward; namely, he had certainly given offense by calling his great comic character Sir John Oldcastle instead of Sir John Falstaff, so perhaps, after all, the original fair copy of 2 *Henry IV* was, relatively speaking, a quite respectable document. It is, however, gratifying to think that Jaggard and Blount have at last been permitted to set up a play from handwritten copy.

The foregoing pages make an effort to simplify the history and classification of the early texts of an important group of Shakespeare's plays—those for which there exist, besides the text in the First Folio, one or more versions in quarto form. I have tried to use fact, and inference from fact, to solve the various problems of interrelationship that arise and, if possible, render them stable elements in the determination of Shakespeare's original text. The current method tends to seek truth by the construction of more or less ingenious invented causes. The result is confusion. One might illustrate this confusion from a recent edition of *King Lear* in which the editor introduces some seventeen different theories, large and small, in his determination of textual relations between quartos and folio. Many of the advocates of these theories are learned and responsible scholars, and the harm done, apart from confusion, is not always great, since if a given theory gets in the way, it is often possible to shove it aside by means of another theory. Certain theories, however, conflict with fact and cannot be bypassed.

One of these is the theory of reporting or memorial reconstruction, which with some scholars has become a process through which all plays passed or might pass, so that a reporter is always conveniently at hand for the removal of almost any obstacle that stands in need of removal. One would be willing to pass the theory by as a sort of romantic relief, if it did not interfere with actuality. The chief offense of this hypothesis, however, is its use as a substitute for a well-known and very powerful agent in the alteration and degeneration of play texts; namely, changes made by actors and managers in the texts of plays when they were acted on the stage. Such changes, sometimes slight and justifiable and sometimes serious, appear in the texts of all plays that were acted on the stage. It becomes necessary, therefore, to say something about this theory of memorial reconstruction. There is no testimony in its favor and no evidence that supports reporting specifically. There is only evidence of the results of faulty memory and of deterioration. Moreover, the theory is unnecessary, since normal conditions and customs explain everything that is to be observed.

Another source of serious error is the use of an outmoded method of textual criticism, priority and derivation being determined solely by agreement without observance of Lachmann's principle of the significance of common error.

What has been suggested is the careful use of a simple factual procedure in an operation that is primarily inductive; indeed, is the ancient argument from effect to cause.

Notes and Index

NOTES

Notes to Chapter 1

1. REFERENCES.—The chief authorities on which these statements are based are the English, mainly nonmathematical works of Einstein; Bertrand Russell, "Logic as the Essence of Philosophy," in *Mysticism and Logic* (London, 1918), and other works by Lord Russell; A. N. Whitehead and Bertrand Russell, *Principia Mathematica* (Cambridge and New York, 1910, 1925), Sections A and B, and other works by Whitehead; J. B. Conant, *Modern Science and the Modern Man* (Garden City, N.Y., 1953); C. I. Lewis and C. H. Langford, *Symbolic Logic* (New York, 1932); and Susanne K. Langer, *An Introduction to Symbolic Logic* (New York, 1953).

2. See Leo Kirschbaum, *Shakespeare and the Stationers* (Columbus, Ohio, 1955); F. P. Wilson, "Shakespeare and the New Bibliography," in *Studies in Retrospect, 1892–1942* (Bibliographical Society, 1945), pp. 76–135.

3. R. B. McKerrow's *Prolegomena for the Oxford Shakespeare: A Study in Editorial Method* (Oxford, 1939) is a very important work, broad in learning, conservative, and eminently practical.

4. Current editions of Shakespeare, such as the New Cambridge, the New Arden, the New Variorum, the Yale, and the Pelican, are usually the product of individual editors and therefore vary from play to play in the degree to which they vitiate Shakespeare's text by adherence to false theories; as also by their misunderstanding of the classification of early texts.

5. For information about the players' efforts to prevent the publication of their plays by entries in the Stationers' Register, see E. K. Chambers, *William Shakespeare* (2 vols., Oxford, 1930), I, 145–50, and Evelyn May Albright, *Dramatic Publication in England, 1580–1640* (New York, 1927), esp. pp. 240, 266.

6. This statement makes no provision for the possibility that stenography may have entered into the production of the quarto of *Henry V*. See note 12 below.

7. See A. N. Whitehead, *Adventures of Ideas*, Mentor Books (New York, 1955), pp. 185–90.

8. See Langer, *An Introduction to Symbolic Logic*; Lewis and Langford, *Symbolic Logic*; and works by Whitehead and Russell (see note 1 above).

9. It is difficult to find an exposition of the new theory of cognition, which is derived from Minkowsky's theory of the space-time continuum. It finds its fullest application in Whitehead's *Process and Reality* (New York, 1929).

10. Inductive reasoning is an old subject and is perhaps best studied in the works of some of the proponents of "Baconian induction," such as James McCosh's *An Examination of Mr. J. S. Mill's Philosophy* (London, 1866) and *The Laws of Discursive Thought* (New York, 1891). See also J. G. Hibben, *Logic, Deductive and Inductive* (1910); Whitehead and Russell, *Principia Mathematica*; and R. W. Bridgman, *The Logic of Modern Physics* (New York, 1927). The following works may also be of assistance: A. N. Whitehead, *Science and the Modern World* (New York, 1926) and G. J. Garraghan, *A Guide to Historical Method* (New York, 1946).

11. It is possible that if Pollard had made a detailed study of *Pericles*, he would have seen that he had to do with a very different document from the four quartos on which he based his hypothesis of pirate actors. Pollard's last work on Shakespeare's text should be consulted. See "Shakespeare's Text," in *A Companion to Shakespeare Studies*, ed. H. Granville-Barker and G. B. Harrison (Cambridge, 1934), pp. 263–86. Pollard here describes various developments of his theory of the bad quartos, but without definite commitment.

12. We know from the familiar statements of Thomas Heywood and Sir George Buck (see Chambers, *William Shakespeare*, I, 147, 159–62) that persons in a position to know believed that shorthand was used in the Elizabethan theater dishonestly to make reports of plays. The best case for the stenographic reproduction of a play by Shakespeare is that presented by H. T. Price for the quarto of *Henry V*. See *The Text of Henry V* (Newcastle-under-Lyme, 1920) and "The Quarto and Folio Texts of Henry V," *Philological Quarterly*, XII (1933), 24–32. The possibility has to be admitted, but the trouble has so far been that the criteria adduced to prove stenographic origin have been generally mnemonic and not exclusively applicable to shorthand reporting and to no other process in the production of texts. It may be that a better logic of research will yet reveal the truth of this matter.

13. Pollard in "Shakespeare's Text" (see *A Companion to Shakespeare Studies*, p. 268, n. 12) attributed the theory of memorial reconstruction to Sir Walter Greg in *Two Elizabethan Stage Abridgments* (Oxford, 1923) (in connection with the text of Greene's *Orlando Furioso*) and to R. Crompton Rhodes in *Studies in the First Folio* (Oxford, 1924). The bibliography of the subject is extensive, but an idea of the theory and of the books and articles dealing with it can be gained from Chambers, *William Shakespeare*, Subject-Index, sub " 'Reported' plays," and from W. W. Greg, *The Editorial Problem in Shakespeare* (Oxford, 1951), esp. pp. 49–101.

14. See Chambers, *William Shakespeare*, I, 156–57, 234–42.

15. See the author's "Textual Degeneration of Elizabethan and Stuart Plays: An Examination of Plays in Manuscript," *The Rice Institute Pamphlet,* XLVI (1960), 71–84.

16. REFERENCES.—J. Q. Adams, "The Quarto of *King Lear* and Shorthand," *Modern Philology,* XXXI (1933), 135–63. Elizabeth Taylor Barnes, "Quarto Irregularity in the Composition of King Lear," unpublished M. A. thesis, University of Missouri, 1953. Chambers, *William Shakespeare,* I, 463–70. Madeleine Doran, "The Text of *King Lear* and Bright's Shorthand," *Modern Philology,* XXXIII (1935), 139–57. G. I. Duthie, *Elizabethan Shorthand and the First Quarto of 'King Lear'* (Oxford, 1949). W. W. Greg, *The Variants in the First Quarto of 'King Lear'* (London, 1940); "The Function of Bibliography in Literary Criticism illustrated in a study of the Text of King Lear," *Neophilologus,* XVIII (1933), 241–62; *The Editorial Problem in Shakespeare,* esp. pp. 88–101; and *The Shakespeare First Folio* (Oxford, 1955), pp. 375–88. *King Lear,* ed. Kenneth Muir (London, 1953). Alice Walker, " 'King Lear'—the 1608 Quarto," *Modern Language Review,* XLVII (1952), 376–78; and *Textual Problems of the First Folio* (Cambridge, 1953), pp. 37–67.

17. Greg, ed., *Henslowe's Diary* (2 vols., London, 1904, 1908), II, 162.

18. *Ibid.,* I, 4.

19. Chambers, *The Elizabethan Stage* (4 vols., Oxford, 1923), II, 114; IV, 25–26.

20. See Barnes, "Quarto Irregularity in the Composition of King Lear."

21. Madeleine Doran, *The Text of King Lear* (Stanford, 1931), pp. 52–68.

22. REFERENCES.—Chambers, *William Shakespeare,* I, 518–28. Philip Edwards, "An Approach to the Problem of Pericles," *Shakespeare Survey,* V, (1952), 25–49. T. S. Graves, "On the Date and Significance of *Pericles,*" *Modern Philology,* XIII (1916), 545–56. Greg, *The Editorial Problem in Shakespeare,* pp. vii, 16–19, 74–75, 106, 170. A. W. Pollard, *Shakespeare Folios and Quartos* (Oxford, 1909), pp. 62, 78–79; and *Shakespeare's Fight with the Pirates* (Cambridge, 1920), p. xxvi. Grace Seiler, "Shakespeare's Part in Pericles," doctoral dissertation, University of Missouri, 1951 (microfilmed). Sina Spiker, "George Wilkins and the Authorship of Pericles," *Studies in Philology,* XXX (1933), 551–70. Laurence Twine, *The Patterne of painefull Aduentures* in *Shakespeare Library,* ed. W. C. Hazlitt (London, 1875), IV, 299–334 (contains "Mr. Collier's Introduction"). H. D. Sykes, "Wilkins and Shakespeare's *Pericles, Prince of Tyre,*" in *Sidelights on Shakespeare* (Stratford-on-Avon, 1919), pp. 143–203. George Wilkins, *The Painful Aduentures of Pericles, Prince of Tyre,* ed. Kenneth Muir (Liverpool, 1953), Introduction, pp. iii–xv, and text.

23. See Chambers, *William Shakespeare,* I, 518 ff. The phraseology of

the entry in the Stationers' Register of May 20, 1608, indicates that the item entered by Edward Blount was an official playbook belonging to the King's company, since it speaks of "A booke called, the booke of Pericles prynce of Tyre." If so, it may have been a staying entry designed to forestall the publication by Henry Gosson of Shakespeare's revision of the old play of Pericles. If this is true, it failed of its purpose.

24. This book was entered in the Stationers' Register to N. How on July 7, 1576, but if it was published at that time, no copy has been preserved. There is also an edition of about 1594.

25. Sykes in "Wilkins and Shakespeare's *Pericles, Prince of Tyre*," pp. 143–203, saw that Shakespeare's play is later than the novel, but the inferences he drew from his observation are not the same as those here presented.

26. See I, i, 162–66; ii, 104–9; iii, 11–24; iv, 57–59, 71–73, 77–81; II, i, 56–58, 60–61, 66–68, 101–15, 165–67 (prose also as verse); III, iii, 1–5, 36–41 (also much misalignment).

27. REFERENCES.—Peter Alexander, "Troilus and Cressida, 1609," *The Library*. 4. ser., IX (1928), 165–68. Chambers, *William Shakespeare*, I, 438–39. Greg, *The Editorial Problem in Shakespeare*, esp. pp. xxiv, 111–14; and *The Shakespeare First Folio*, pp. 66–67, 338–50, 445–58. Pollard, *Shakespeare's Folios and Quartos*, pp. 56–58, 65–67, 76–78, 116, 136–37. S. A. Tannenbaum, "A Critique of the Text of *Troilus and Cressida*," Shakespeare Association, *Bulletin*, IX (1934), 55–74, 125–44, 198–214. Alice Walker, *Textual Problems of the First Folio*, pp. 68–93. Philip Williams, "Shakespeare's *Troilus and Cressida*: The Relationship of Quarto to Folio," *Studies in Bibliography*, III (1950–51), 131–43.

28. I, 438–45.

29. It is necessary to proceed with caution in setting up hard and fast divisions between the work of the printers of the First Folio. Willoughby, who made the original study of the spelling habits of the printers (A and B) of the folio, is by no means so positive in his classification as later workers. He seems fairly confident in his identification of the work of A, but does not commit himself beyond his findings with reference to B. See E. E. Willoughby, *The Printing of the First Folio of Shakespeare* (Bibliographical Society, 1932).

30. REFERENCES.—K. W. Cameron, "Othello, Quarto 1, Reconsidered," *PMLA*, XLVII (1932), 671–83; and "The Text of *Othello*. An Analysis," *PMLA*, XLIX (1934), 762–96. Chambers, *William Shakespeare*, I, 457–63. Greg, *The Editorial Problem in Shakespeare*, pp. xxiv, xxix, xxxi–xxxii, xxxvi, 108–12, 173–4; and *The Shakespeare First Folio*, pp. 357–74. McKerrow, *Prolegomena for the Oxford Shakespeare*, pp. 13–14. R. Crompton Rhodes, *Shakespeare's First Folio* (Oxford, 1923), esp. pp. 117–19. Walker, *Textual Problems of the First Folio*, pp. 138–61; and

"The 1622 Quarto and the First Folio Text of *Othello*," *Shakespeare Survey*, 5, 16–24.

31. REFERENCES.—Chambers, *William Shakespeare*, I, 375–84. Greg, *The Editorial Problem in Shakespeare*, pp. xvi, xxiv-xxv, xxxvi, xxxix, xlii, 114–17, 128–30, 174–76, 180–81; and *The Shakespeare First Folio*, pp. 64–65, 262–76; Harold Jenkins, *The Structural Problems in Shakespeare's Henry the Fourth* (London, 1956). A. E. Morgan, *Some Problems of Shakespeare's "King Henry IV*," Shakespeare Association Papers (Oxford, 1924). *The First Part of the History of Henry IV*, ed. J. Dover Wilson, The New Shakespeare (Cambridge, 1946). *Henry IV*, Part I, ed. S. B. Hemingway, New Variorum Edition (Philadelphia, 1936), esp. pp. 495–501. *The Second Part of the History of Henry IV*, ed. M. A. Shaaber, New Variorum Edition (Philadelphia, 1940), esp. pp. 645–50. *The Second Part of the History of Henry IV*, ed. J. Dover Wilson, The New Shakespeare (Cambridge, 1946). *Shakespeare's Play of King Henry the Fourth, Printed from a Contemporary Manuscript*, ed. J. O. Halliwell, Shakespeare Society, *Publications*, XIV (1845). Walker, *Textual Problems of the First Folio*, pp. 94–120.

32. See *Shakespeare's Play of King Henry the Fourth*, ed. Halliwell, in the preceding note.

33. This opinion is mistaken, since it rests on a methodological error in textual criticism. This will be explained in the third chapter below, where the textual relation between the Dering play and *1* and *2 Henry IV* will be further considered.

34. Ind., 29–32; I, i, 7–11, 41–42, 60–115, 129–33, 136–56, 163–65, 180–86, 212–15.

Notes to Chapter 2

1. The New Variorum edition (p. 515), for example, would introduce some such operation to account for a certain literary finish.

2. REFERENCES.—Chambers, *The Elizabethan Stage*, II, esp. 95; and *William Shakespeare*, I, 338–475. L. A. Cummings, "Abridgement in the 1597 Quarto of Romeo and Juliet," unpublished M. A. thesis, University of Missouri, 1952. G. I. Duthie, "The Text of Shakespeare's *Romeo and Juliet*," *Studies in Bibliography* (University of Virginia), IV (1951–52), 3–29. Greg, *The Editorial Problem in Shakespeare*, pp. xvi, 61–66, 75, 103, 116, 162–64; and *Shakespeare's First Folio*, pp. 63, 110–14, 225–35. Greta Hjort, "The Good and Bad Quartos of 'Romeo and Juliet' and 'Love's Labour's Lost,' " *Modern Language Review*, XXI (1926), 140–46. H. R. Hoppe, *The Bad Quarto of Romeo and Juliet* (Ithaca, 1948); and "The First Quarto Version of *Romeo and Juliet* (II, vi and IV, v, 43 ff.)," *Review of English Studies*, XIV (1938), 271–84. J. T. Murray, *English Dramatic*

Companies (2 vols., London, 1910), II, esp. 91. *Romeo and Juliet*, ed. J. Dover Wilson and G. I. Duthie, The New Shakespeare (Cambridge, 1955), pp. 112–18. *Romeo and Juliet*, ed. H. H. Furness, New Variorum edition (Philadelphia, 1871). Sidney Thomas, "The First Two Quartos of *Romeo and Juliet*," *Review of English Studies*, XXV (1949), 110–14. J. Dover Wilson, "The New Way with Shakespeare's Texts," *Shakespeare Survey*, VIII (1955), 81–99.

3. See McKerrow, *Prolegomena for the Oxford Shakespeare*, esp. pp. 6–18.

4. See Murray, *English Dramatic Companies*, II, 105; Chambers, *Elizabethan Stage*, II, 195.

5. See McKerrow, "The Elizabethan Printer and Dramatic Manuscripts," *Library*, XII (1931), 253–75.

6. With reference to the defensible state of the last scenes of the first quarto of *Romeo and Juliet*, see Wilson, "The New Way with Shakespeare's Texts," *Shakespeare Survey*, 8.

7. REFERENCES.—William Bracy, *The Merry Wives of Windsor*, University of Missouri Studies (Columbia, Mo., 1952). Chambers, *William Shakespeare*, I, 425. P. A. Daniel, Introduction to *Shakespeare's Merry Wives of Windsor: The First Quarto, 1602*, Griggs Facsimile (London, 1888). W. W. Greg, ed., *Shakespeare's Merry Wives of Windsor, 1602* (Oxford, 1910); Introduction to *The Merry Wives of Windsor, 1602*, Shakespeare Association Quarto Facsimiles, No. 3 (London, 1939), esp. pp. 70–72; and *The Shakespeare First Folio*, pp. 334–37. Leslie Hotson, *Shakespeare versus Shallow* (London, 1931), *passim*. A. W. Pollard, *Shakespeare Folios and Quartos, passim*. A. W. Pollard and J. Dover Wilson, "The Merry Wives of Windsor," *Times Literary Supplement*, August 8, 1919, p. 420. J. S. Smart, *Shakespeare: Truth and Tradition* (London, 1928), esp. pp. 40–43, 95–100. *The Merry Wives of Windsor*, ed. J. Dover Wilson, The New Shakespeare (Cambridge, 1921), pp. 93–101.

8. REFERENCES.—Chambers, *William Shakespeare*, I, 408–25; and *The Elizabethan Stage*, III, esp. 486–87. G. I. Duthie, *The "Bad" Quarto of Hamlet: A Critical Study* (Cambridge, 1941). Frank G. Hubbard, *The First Quarto Edition of Shakespeare's Hamlet* (Madison, 1920). H. D. Gray, "The First Quarto of *Hamlet*," *Modern Language Review*, X (1915), 171–80; and "Reconstruction of a Lost Play," *Philological Quarterly*, VII (1928), 254–74. Greg, *The Editorial Problem in Shakespeare*, esp. pp. 64–70. *Hamlet*, ed. J. Dover Wilson, The New Shakespeare (Cambridge, 1936). C. H. Herford and W. H. Widgery, *The First Quarto Edition of Hamlet: Two Essays* (London, 1880). J. M. Robertson, *The Problem of Hamlet* (London, 1919). L. L. Schücking, *Zum Problem der Überlieferung des Hamlet-Textes* (Leipzig, 1931). E. E. Stoll, *Hamlet: An Historical and Comparative Study* (Minneapolis, 1919). *The Tragedy of Hamlet*,

ed. Thomas Marc Parrott and Hardin Craig (Princeton, 1938). B. A. P. Van Dam, *The Text of Shakespeare's Hamlet* (London, 1924). J. Dover Wilson, "Spelling and Misprints in the 2nd Quarto of *Hamlet*," *Essays and Studies by the Members of the English Association*, X (1924); and *The Manuscript of Shakespeare's Hamlet* (2 vols., Cambridge, 1934).

9. See the author's "Revised Elizabethan Quartos: An Attempt to Form a Class," *Studies in the English Renaissance Drama in memory of Karl Julius Holzknecht* (New York, 1959), pp. 43–57.

10. See McKerrow, "The Elizabethan Printer and Dramatic Manuscripts," pp. 253–75.

11. See books by Hubbard and Stoll as listed in note 8 above.

12. See Leo Kirschbaum, "A Census of Bad Quartos," *Review of English Studies*, XIV (1938), 20–43.

13. The fact that Q1 is a version of the text revised into the form of Q2 disposes of the *ad hoc* argument that the compositor of Q2 resorted to a printed copy of Q1 in setting up Q2. Why should not an original and a revision of it closely resemble each other in certain places, as these texts do?

14. This question will be considered in Chapter 3 below.

15. REFERENCES.—Peter Alexander, *Shakespeare's "Henry VI" and "Richard III"* (Cambridge, 1929); and "*II Henry VI* and the Copy for 'The Contention' (1594)," *Times Literary Supplement*, October 9, 1924, pp. 629–30, and correspondence. C. F. Tucker Brooke, *The Authorship of the Second and Third Parts of "King Henry the Sixth"* (New Haven, 1912) and the same author's editions of *1, 2* and *3 Henry VI* in the Yale Shakespeare. C. F. Denny, "The Sources of *1 Henry VI* as an Indication of Revision," *Philological Quarterly*, XVI (1937) 225–48. Allison Gaw, *The Origin and Development of "1 Henry VI"* (Los Angeles, 1926). Madeleine Doran, *Henry VI, Parts II and III: Their Relation to the "Contention" and the "True Tragedy"* (Iowa City, 1928). J. B. Henneman, "The Episodes in *1 Henry VI*," *PMLA*, XV (1921), 290–320. John Jordan, "The Reporter of *Henry VI, Part 2*," *PMLA*, LXIV (1949) 1089–1113. Lucille King, "The Use of Hall's Chronicles in the Folio and Quarto Texts of *Henry VI*," *Philological Quarterly*, XIII (1934), 321–32; and "Text Sources of the Folio and the Quarto *Henry VI*," *PMLA*, LI (1936), 702–18. R. B. McKerrow, "A Note on 'Henry VI, Part II' and the Contention of York and Lancaster," *Review of English Studies*, IX (1933), 157–69. Josephine A. Pearce, "An Earlier Talbot Epitaph," *Modern Language Notes*, LIX (1944), 327–29. H. T. Price on the quarto of *Henry V* (see p. 120, note 12 above); C. T. Prouty, *The Contention and Shakespeare's 2 Henry VI* (New Haven, 1954). J. Dover Wilson, editions of *1, 2* and *3 Henry VI*, New Shakespeare (Cambridge, 1952).

16. See the author's article, "Relation of the First Quarto Version to

the First Folio Version of Shakespeare's *Henry V*," *Philological Quarterly*, VI (1927), 225–34.

17. See Chambers, *William Shakespeare*, II, 188–89; I, 281–89.

18. See Tucker Brooke's edition of *1 Henry VI*, Yale Shakespeare (New Haven, 1918), pp. 124–25. See also article by Josephine A. Pearce listed in note 15 above.

19. See articles listed in note 15 above.

20. "Text Sources of the Folio and Quarto *Henry VI*," *loc. cit.* (n. 15).

21. Professor Prouty offers no opinion on the relation between *3 Henry VI* and the *True Tragedy*, although this subject enters frequently into the various critical writings he discusses.

22. Since *1 Henry VI* shows evidence of revision apparently intended to establish it as the first member of the trilogy, it may well be that its origin, like that of *2* and *3 Henry VI*, was the revision of an older dramatic treatment of the subject. The form of the Talbot scenes (IV, v–vi), the fate of Joan of Arc (V, iii–iv), and some other features suggest some such relation. For factual matters see Chambers, *William Shakespeare*, I, 289–93; II, 188.

Notes to Chapter 3

1. See J. E. Sandys, *A History of Classical Scholarship* (3 vols., Cambridge, 1903–8), III, esp. 127–31; Paul Maas, *Textual Criticism*, trans. Barbara Flower (Oxford, 1950); A. C. Clark, *The Descent of Manuscripts* (Oxford, 1918); and articles by J. P. Postgate in *Encyclopædia Britannica*, 13th Ed., and in J. E. Sandys, *A Companion to Latin Studies*.

2. See the author's "Revised Elizabethan Quartos: An Attempt to form a Class," *Studies in the English Renaissance Drama*, pp. 43–57.

3. The most important work in advocacy of the printing of folio texts from quartos is W. W. Greg, *The Shakespeare First Folio* (Oxford, 1955). Closer detail, however, is to be found in special studies, such as Alice Walker, *Textual Problems of the First Folio* (Cambridge, 1953), in articles in learned journals, and in many editions of the plays concerned—The New Shakespeare (Cambridge University Press), the New Arden Shakespeare (Methuen, London), the Yale Shakespeare (New Haven), and certain volumes in the New Variorum. The weight of authority is thus heavily on the side of printing from quartos.

4. Sir Edmund Chambers in *William Shakespeare: A Study of Facts and Problems* gives a particularized account and provides an extensive bibliography that can be easily supplemented with later publications.

5. No printed quarto that has been put to such use has been found. The copy of *A Looking Glass for London and England* discovered by the late C. R. Baskervill and described by him in *Modern Philology*, XXX, 29–51, is an altogether different document from those called for in the theory. A

few passages have been canceled, and there are a few casual notes in writing, but, except for omissions, the text itself is practically without modification.

6. *The Tragedy of King Richard II, Printed for the 3rd time by Valentine Simmes,* ed. A. W. Pollard (London, 1916).

7. H. E. Hasker, "The Copy for the First Folio *Richard II," Studies in Bibliography,* V (1953), 53–72.

8. It is interesting to note that in the few cases, such as the sixth quarto of *Richard II,* in which a printer has continued his issue of quarto texts after the folio was issued, the same series of printers' corrections and miscorrections continue, and it is only the fixed date of 1623 that prevents scholars from deriving the folio text from quartos that were not published until after 1623.

9. For an account of certain passages in the play that occur in both an early and a revised form and for other evidences of revision, see *Love's Labour's Lost,* ed. J. Dover Wilson, The New Shakespeare (Cambridge, 1923), pp. 105–16. The occurrence of such repeated passages would indicate that Shakespeare in his revision was working on an original manuscript that would thus have been destroyed in the process. This in turn would render doubtful the speculation that there was ever a so-called "bad" quarto of *Love's Labour's Lost.* See Greg, *The Shakespeare First Folio,* pp. 219–21.

10. See *Prolegomena for the Oxford Shakespeare,* esp. pp. 6–18.

11. See *Love's Labour's Lost,* ed. J. Dover Wilson, pp. 97–109.

12. See Greg, *The Shakespeare First Folio,* pp. 220–23; Chambers, *William Shakespeare,* I, 333–35.

13. See *Much Ado about Nothing,* ed. J. Dover Wilson, The New Shakespeare (Cambridge, 1923), pp. 102–7.

14. See Chambers, *William Shakespeare,* I, 144–48, 384–88.

15. See Chambers, *William Shakespeare,* II, 330–32.

16. See *A Midsummer-Night's Dream,* ed. J. Dover Wilson, The New Shakespeare (Cambridge, 1924), pp. 80–92; Chambers, *William Shakespeare,* II, 360–62.

17. There are, however, important studies by recent scholars: David L. Patrick, *The Textual History of Richard III* (Stanford, 1936); Alice Walker, "*Richard III*" in *Textual Problems of the First Folio* (Cambridge, 1953), pp. 13–36; and *Richard III,* ed. J. Dover Wilson (Cambridge, 1954), pp. 140–60. The opinion to be considered and questioned in these and other works is that the quarto version is the product of a suppository process called memorial reconstruction.

18. Introduction to the Griggs facsimile of Richard III, Quarto One.

19. *The Shakespeare First Folio,* pp. 191–92.

20. "Quartos und Folio von Richard III," *Shakespeare-Jahrbuch,* XV (1880), 301–24.

21. See Patrick, esp. pp. 105–32.

22. *Some Problems of Shakespeare's* "Henry the Fourth" (London, 1924).

23. The following collation was based on the printed version of the Dering play, *Shakespeare's Play of King Henry the Fourth, Printed from a Contemporary Manuscript,* ed. J. O. Halliwell, Shakespeare Society, *Publications,* Vol. XIV (1845). This collation must be regarded as tentative, since there has not been time or opportunity to check it against the manuscript. It counts only what seemed to be clear cases.

24. See J. Dover Wilson's edition of *2 Henry IV* in the New Shakespeare, pp. 115-23; New Variorum edition, pp. 488-94; Greg, *The Editorial Problem in Shakespeare,* pp. 115-16, and *The Shakespeare First Folio,* pp. 267-72; Alice Walker, *Textual Problems of the First Folio,* pp. 94-120; and Chambers, *William Shakespeare,* I, 379-83.

INDEX

Act to Restrain the Abuses of Players, 41–42

All's Well that Ends Well, 5

Alteration and deterioration of plays on the stage, 9–10, 14–15, 54–55, 88–89, 92–94, 101

Belleforest, François de (1530–83), *Histoires tragiques*, 80

bestrafte Brudermord, Der, 79–80; see also *Hamlet*

Bibliographical method, 4–9, 94–95; and *Pericles*, 19–20, 23–26; and *M.W.W.*, 66–70; and *Ham.*, 77–78, 81–82; and *1, 2, 3 Hen. VI*, 84–85; and *3 Hen. VI*, 88–89; and *Rich. II*, 97–98; and *Lear*, 98–99; and *L.L.L.*, 104–5; and *Rich. III*, 110–11

Bracy, William, 67, 70, 75

Brooke, C. F. Tucker, 84

Butler, Joseph (1692–1752), Bishop, 1–2

Cambridge edition, the (1865), 95–96

Chambers, E. K., 9–10, 21, 26, 110

Classification: discussions of, 3–7, 83, 88–89, 93–95, 101–2, 117–18; *Lear*, 10–17; *Pericles*, 21–26; *T. & C.*, 26–29; *Oth.*, 37–41; *1, 2 Hen. IV*, 45–46; *R. & J.*, 54–60, 62–63; *M.W.W.*, 65–68, 74–75; *Ham.*, 76–78, 80–81; *1 Hen. VI*, 85–86; *M. of V.*, 107–8; *1 Hen. IV*, 113–14

Collier, J. P., 21

Condell, Henry (d. 1627), 66, 96, 115

Contention betwixt the two famous Houses of Yorke and Lancaster, The First Part of the, 83–84; see also under *Henry VI*

Coriolanus, 27

Cotton, Roger (fl. 1596), *An Armor of Proofe*, 84

Crompton, Richard (fl. 1573–99), *The Mansion of Magnanimitie*, 84

Cummings, L. A., 55–60

Daniel, P. A., 110

Denny, C. F., 85

Dering, Sir Edward (1598–1644), 43–44, 49–50

Dering ms., 43–52, 110–15; see also under *Henry IV*

Doran, Madeleine, 14

Dramatic companies, Elizabethan: and *Lear*, 11, 14; and *Pericles*, 17; and *R. & J.*, 54–55; and *M.W.W.*, 65, 67–69; and *Ham.*, 75–77; and *Much Ado*, 106; and *M.N.D.*, 109

Famous Victories of Henry V, The, 88–89

Fletcher, John (1579–1625), *The Spanish Curate*, 44

Gesta Romanorum, 18

Gower, John (1325–1408), version of *Apollonius of Tyre*, 18–19

Graves, T. S., 24

Greene, Robert (1560?–1592), *A Groatsworth of Wit*, 84

Greg, W. W., 110

Halliwell (Halliwell-Phillipps), J. O., 43

Hamlet, 75–83, 103–4; versions, 75–77; Q2, 76–78; Q1, 77–81; German Hamlet (*Der bestrafte Brudermord*), 79–80; summary, 82–83; mentions, 5, 8, 61, 88, 101, 105

Hart, Alfred, 21

Hasker, H. F., 97

Heminge, John (1556?–1630), 66, 96, 115

Henry IV: parts 1 and 2 in relation to the Dering version, 43–50; Dering manuscript, 43–45; comparison of plots, 44–52; texts, 46; *2 Hen. IV*, revision, 51–52; textual study of the Dering version, 112–15; summary, 112–16; mentions, 85, 101, 110

Henry V, 8, 83, 85

Henry VI, parts 1, 2, and 3, 83–88, 102; *2, 3 Hen. VI* in relation to *The Contention* and *The True Tragedy*, 83–84; *1 Hen. VI*, theory of revision, 85–86; *3 Hen. VI* and *The True Tragedy* compared, 86–88

Henslowe's *Diary*, 11

Holinshed, Raphael (d. ca. 1580), *Chronicles*, 49, 51, 88

Hotson, Leslie, 67

Induction and deduction, 1–7, 53–54, 83, 88–89, 91–95; and *1, 2 Hen. IV*, 44–45, 115–17; and *R. & J.*, 54–56, 101; and *M.W.W.*, 66–67; and *Ham.*, 75, 79–81; and *1, 2, 3 Hen. VI*, 85–86; and *Lear*, 98–99; and *L.L.L.*, 104–5

Julius Caesar, 28

King, Lucille, 85

King Lear, 5, 37, 102; quarto of 1608 misclassified, 10–17

King Leir, The True Chronicle History of, 11–12

Lachmann, Karl, 90–95, 99–100, 102

Love's Labour's Lost, 101, 103–5

Macbeth, 88

McKerrow, R. B., 3–4, 25–26, 105

Measure for Measure, 23

Memorial reconstruction, theory of, 13, 117–18

Merchant of Venice, The, 101–2, 107–8

Meres, Francis (1565–1647), *Palladis Tamia*, 44

Merry Wives of Windsor, The, 8, 83, 88; quarto and folio versions compared, 65–75

Midsummer-Night's Dream, A, 101, 108–9

Mirror for Magistrates, A, 86

Morgan, A. E., 44, 113

Much Ado about Nothing, 101, 105–7

Nashe, Thomas (1567–1601): *The Isle of Dogs*, 67; *Pierce Penilesse his Supplication to the Divell*, 86

Occam, William of (1300?–1349?), 116
Othello, 37–43, 103

Patrick, David L., 110
Peano, Giuseppe, 6
Pearce, Josephine A., 84
Pericles, 3, 8, 37; misclassification of quarto text, 17–26
Plays, supply of to actors and publishers: discussed, 3–4; Lear, 13–14; Pericles, 23, 25–26; T. & C., 26–29; Oth., 40–41, 43; R. & J., 54–55, 61; M.W.W., 67–69; Ham., 75–81; Hen. V, 83; 1, 2, 3 Hen. VI, 85–86; Much Ado, 106; M. of V., 107; Rich. III, 110–11; see also Alteration; Quarto and folio texts; and plays by name
Pollard, A. W., 5–9, 21, 66–67, 97–98
Price, H. T., 83
Printers and publishers, Elizabethan and Jacobean: Lear, 11, 98–99; Pericles, 17–18, 25–26; T. & C., 27–28, 36–37; Oth., 40–41; R. & J., 61; Ham., 75, 80; quarto and folio texts, 94–95; Rich. II, 104; M. of V., 107; M.N.D., 109; Rich. III, 110; 1 Hen. IV, 115
Prouty, C. T., 85–86

Quarto and folio texts, 3, 92–94; Lear, 14–16; Pericles, 23; T. & C., 27–29; R. & J., 55–56; M.W.W., 74–75; Ham., 80–81; printing of, 94–95; Rich. III, 109–11

Revision: Lear, 14; Pericles, 19–20; Oth., 42; 2 Hen. IV, 51;

M.W.W., 74–75; Ham., 75–76, 82–83; 1, 2, 3 Hen. VI, 83–85; revised plays as folio copy, 88–89, 93–95, 101–6, 108–9, 113
Reprinted quartos, 94–7; liberties taken by printers, 103–4, 115
Richard II, 85, 96–98, 102, 110
Richard III, 85, 102, 109–11
Romeo and Juliet, 8, 27–29; Q1 misclassified, 54–55; abridgment, 55–59; actor economy, 57–60; special features, 61–65; Q2 printed from foul papers of a revision, 61, 81, 88, 95–96, 101–2, 105

Saxo Grammaticus (1150?–1220?), Danish historian, 80
Schmidt, Alexander, 111
Seiler, Grace, 19–25
Sidney, Sir Philip (1554–86), Arcadia, minor plot of Lear, 12–13

Textual criticism of Shakespeare's quartos, 90–117; emendation and Lachmann's doctrine, 90–91, 95–96; effects of corrections in reprinted quartos, 100–102, 112–16
Theories, erroneous or incomplete, 2–3, 53–54, 117–18; the "bad" quartos, 7–10; report theory in Lear, 13, 16–17; Dering ms. and 2 Hen. IV, 49–51; Q1 Ham., 73–83; folio text of Rich. II, 96–97
Timon of Athens, 28
Titus Andronicus, 27
Troilus and Cressida, 5, 26–37, 103; texts, 26–29; omissions, 29–31; stage directions, 31–33; language, 33–35; variants, 35–37

True Tragedie of Richard Duke of Yorke, The, 83–84; *see also under Henry VI*

Twine, Lawrence (fl. 1576), *The Pattern of painefull Aduentures of Apollonius of Tyre*, 18–20

Walker, Alice, 110

Wilkins, George (fl. 1605–8), *The Painfull Adventures of Pericles Prince of Tyre*, 18–20, 24–25

Wilson, J. Dover, 75, 77, 105–6, 110, 116